Practise Your Spelling Skills

THIRD EDITION

4

John Rose

Pearson Australia
(a division of Pearson Australia Group Pty Ltd)
707 Collins Street, Melbourne, Victoria 3008
PO Box 23360, Melbourne, Victoria 8012
www.pearson.com.au

Copyright © Pearson Australia 2006
(a division of Pearson Australia Group Pty Ltd)

First published 2006 by Pearson Australia
Reprinted 2007, 2008, 2009, 2011 (twice), 2012, 2013, 2014, 2015

Edited by Anne McKenna
Cover and interior design by Kim Ferguson-Somerton
Illustrations by Ash Oswald
Cover image by Getty Images
Produced by Pearson Australia
Printed in Australia by the SOS Print + Media Group

ISBN 978-0-7339-7820-3

Pearson Australia Group Pty Ltd   ABN 40 004 245 943

Contents

Spelling and writing

This spelling program, which groups words according to common visual patterns, has been prepared in response to a defined need. Spelling is one of the sub-skills of writing along with appropriate syntactical structures, punctuation, vocabulary development and handwriting. Writing activities in the primary school should, wherever possible, emphasise the inter-relatedness of these sub-skills as well as the inter-relatedness of the other areas of language—listening, speaking and reading.

For written communication children need to have the desire and ability to express themselves through writing their ideas, thoughts, feelings and knowledge with increasing confidence and skill.

Spelling ability grows most effectively when viewed as an integral part of the total language program, and is developed through a continuous program that recognises both increasing ability and changing interests of the writer.

As children develop the desire to communicate their ideas in writing, they need skills in spelling which can be provided systematically. The skills and the appropriate experiences can, in many instances, go hand in hand.

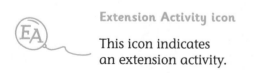

Extension Activity icon

This icon indicates an extension activity.

In this book …

This book contains 36 units, four of which are revision units. Most of the remaining 32 units begin with a list of words that contain a common visual element. Several activities in the unit are related specifically to these list words to ensure children have plenty of practice spelling the words as well as understanding word meanings and usage. There is also a variety of more general activities, including word searches, puzzles and crosswords. A number of extension activities have also been built into the units.

In approximately every second unit a 'Something to remember' section covers basic spelling and grammar rules, with at least two activities for the students to apply the rule in practice. In Book 4 some of the areas covered include the various ways of forming plurals, homonyms, homographs, compound words, contractions, synonyms and antonyms.

Other units in Book 4 include an Olympic Games theme, Australian and New Zealand cities, and two units covering commonly misspelt words. Challenge words are also included in a number of units to further extend fast-finishers. All of the list and challenge words are provided at the end of the book on pages 110 to 112. A helpful list of word extensions (based on the words in the book) from which many new activities could emanate is also provided on pages 113 to 115.

The units in this book are sequential in nature, covering the basic spelling requirements for students at this level. It has been designed to allow for those teachers who wish to teach spelling as a discrete subject, and for those who wish to apply the words in various writing applications. The extensive section at the back of the book covering word extensions is included for this purpose.

Word list with common letter pattern highlighted

Common letter pattern

'Something to remember' focuses upon another aspect of spelling

Extension activities indicated by icon

Activities in which children explore and practise the word list words

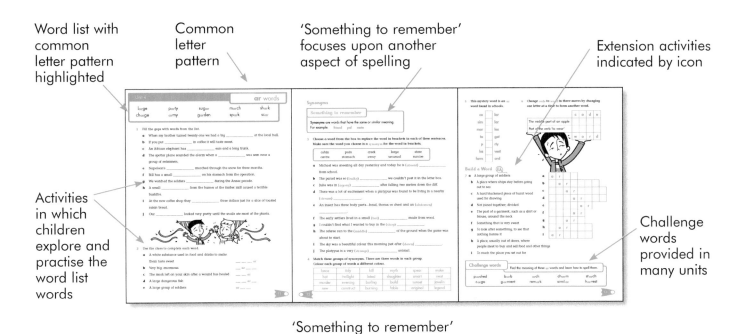

Challenge words provided in many units

'Something to remember' focuses upon another aspect of spelling

Word list for theme unit (two in book). There are also two units on commonly misspelt words.

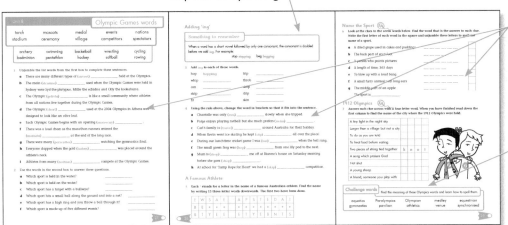

Activities in which children explore and practise the word list and other words

Challenge words provided in many units

Revision unit (four in book)

Activities in which children explore and apply knowledge of words from earlier units

a–e and i–e words

rake	tale	skate	prize	alive	invite
awake	lane	chase	size	fire	inside
snake	became	plane	while	shine	outside
sale	plate	aeroplane	awhile	white	beside

1 **Fill the gaps with a–e words from the list.**

a The long brown _____ slithered through the grass.

b When the scores were level, with only two minutes of the match left to play, the crowd

_____ very excited.

c My brother bought a set of very old and rare books at the white elephant

_____ .

d The police car travelled at high speeds during the _____ .

e The _____ landed at Wellington airport.

f In autumn we often need to _____ the leaves.

g A carpenter uses a _____ to smooth the wood.

h Drivers were not allowed to park their cars along the narrow _____.

i Samantha said she stayed _____ all night because she thought she heard

a mouse in her wardrobe.

j I like to _____ on ice but I often fall over.

k The biscuits on the _____ were soon eaten by the hungry children.

l My uncle Jessie told me a _____ about a shipwrecked sailor.

2 **Write a sentence for each of these words to show what they mean.**

sale _____

sail _____

plane _____

plain _____

tale _____

tail _____

3 Fill the gaps with i–e words from the list.

a That spider at the bottom of the glass jar is still _____.

b It is very cloudy this morning but later the sun should _____.

c If you wait _____ I'll help you move that heavy box.

d The campers pitched their tent _____ the river.

e Nobody was in the building when it caught on _____.

f My brother wears a _____ eight shoe.

g Bulldog footballers wear red, _____ and blue jumpers.

h The gigantic pumpkin that my grandfather grew won first _____ at the show.

i When it is my birthday I will _____ you to my party.

k I watched the All Blacks train _____ my brother went swimming.

j The wind is blowing very strongly _____ .

4 Use the clues to complete each word.

a The colour of snow ___ ___ i ___ e

b The flame, light and heat made by something burning ___ i ___ e

c A reward for doing something well ___ ___ i ___ e

d Within; not outside ___ ___ ___ i ___ e

e Living; not dead ___ ___ i ___ e

f To give out a bright light ___ ___ i ___ e

g During that time; as long as ___ ___ i ___ e

5 Use the clue to complete each word.

a To glide over ice   ___ ___ a ___ e

b A reptile that is often poisonous   ___ ___ a ___ e

c A pole with a comb-like crossbar used for smoothing loose soil   ___ a ___ e

d A shallow bowl from which food is eaten   ___ ___ a ___ e

e A tool used for smoothing wood   ___ ___ a ___ e

f Not asleep   ___ ___ a ___ e

g Narrow road or street   ___ a ___ e

6 Follow the boxes to find five list words.

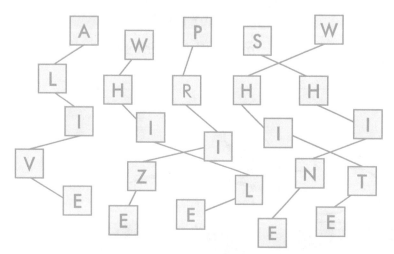

_____

_____

_____

_____

_____

These a–e Words are Ace! (EA)

7 **a** To move quickly in a contest or speed   ___ ace

b A thing that holds parts together or in place   ___ ___ ace

c A place with nothing in it   ___ ___ ace

d House where a king or queen lives   ___ ___ ___ ace

e A short prayer said before a meal   ___ ___ ace

f A long stick with a metal ornament on top   ___ ace

g To put in a particular position   ___ ___ ace

ay words

yesterday	always	replay	spray	crayon
holiday	display	stray	mayor	highway

1 **Fill the gaps with words from the list.**

a Australia Day is a national _____ celebrated in January of each year.

b The skeleton of the large dinosaur was on _____ in the museum.

c As we were driving along the _____ we counted the number of trucks that passed.

d Today I will have to finish the painting that I started _____.

e My baby sister scribbled on my book with a red _____.

f Whenever we plan a trip to the zoo it _____ seems to rain.

g We watched the _____ of the netball match on TV.

h The ranger put the _____ dog in her van and took it to the lost dogs' home.

i My uncle was elected as _____ of the city.

j When the waves hit against the rocks we were covered with _____.

Block Out

2 **Every time you see a list word cross it out. You'll be left with a message giving you some information.**

the	holiday	koala	is	always
replay	called	Australia's	stray	teddy
bear	but	spray	it	is
yesterday	not	a	bear	at
all	display	it	mayor	is
crayon	a	highway	marsupial	which
means	holiday	the	mother	always
display	carries	yesterday	her	mayor
replay	spray	young	in	crayon
stray	a	display	pouch	replay

Homonyms

3   How many different meanings for the word stall can you find in a dictionary?
After each sentence below, write the correct meaning of the word stall.

a   The cold weather made the car stall at the traffic lights.

_____

b   After the race the horse was led back to the stall.

_____

c   The fruit stall was near the back of the market.

_____

4   Find three meanings for the word shell. Write three sentences to show the differences
in meaning.

_____

_____

_____

Multiple Meanings

5   Read each of the sentences below. Using a dictionary to help you, write out the meaning of
the word in green print.

a   Richard tried to put the cards back in order. _____

b   The telephone was out of order. _____

c   The police help to keep law and order. _____

d   Dad is going to order a large cake for Mum's fortieth birthday. _____

An 'ay' Crossword

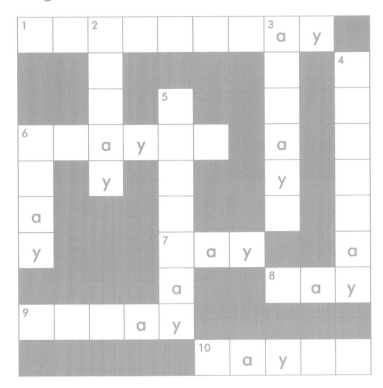

Across

1 The day before today
6 Something used to draw with
7 The time between sunrise and sunset
8 Money you get for the work you have done
9 Fine drops of liquid
10 A person chosen to be leader of a town council

Down

2 To wander away in the wrong direction
3 At all times; forever
4 A major road for cars, trucks, etc.
5 A time when you do not have to go to school
6 Soft, sticky earth

Words in a Word

7 **The middle three letters of each of these five-letter words make a short word. What are the five-letter words?**

   a The opening in your face which you use for speaking and eating
   b The material used to write on or wrap parcels in
   c To take something which belongs to someone else
   d To move smoothly down or along on something
   e A very small person with a magic wand
   f Drops of water that come from your eyes when you are hurt or sad
   g The platform in a theatre or hall where people act, sing or speak
   h The colour of snow
   i To move forward on your hands and knees
   j Sheets of paper in a book, newspaper or magazine

a		o	u	t	
b		a	p	e	
c		t	e	a	
d		l	i	d	
e		a	i	r	
f		e	a	r	
g		t	a	g	
h		h	i	t	
i		r	a	w	
j		a	g	e	

ee words

seem	knee	wheel	coffee	steep
needle	between	speech	agree	sweep

1 Use the clues to complete each list word.

a A large flat circle of wood or metal that helps cars,

bicycles, etc. move along   ___ ___ ee ___

b A hot drink made from roasted beans   ___ ___ ___ ___ ee

c The joint in the middle of your leg   ___ ___ ee

d A long thin piece of metal used for sewing   ___ ee ___ ___ ___

e To use a brush to clean the floor   ___ ___ ee ___

f To appear to be   ___ ee ___

g In the middle of two things   ___ ___ ___ ___ ee ___

h Sloping sharply   ___ ___ ee ___

i To be of the same opinion   ___ ___ ___ ee

j The power of speaking   ___ ___ ee ___ ___

2 Use these letters to make as many ee words as you can.

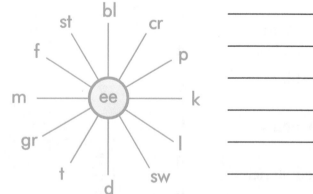

_____ _____ _____

_____ _____ _____

_____ _____ _____

_____ _____ _____

_____ _____ _____

_____ _____ _____

_____ _____ _____

3 Circle the ee in each of these list words.

between   speech   coffee   needle   agree

Now write these words in alphabetical order.

_____

4 Put ee in the correct place in each group of letters to make a word.

a stp

s _____

b betwn

b_____

c tth

t _____

d toff

t _____

e bld

b _____

f btle

b _____

g whl

w _____

h grn

g _____

i spch

s _____

j slp

s _____

k frze

f _____

l chse

c _____

5 Fill the gaps with words from the list.

a The tennis player had an operation on his left _____.

b Remi has four teaspoons of sugar in his _____!

c Dad broke the _____ on the sewing machine.

d The mayor made a long _____ at the opening of the library.

e It was hard towing the caravan up the _____ hill.

f I had to sit _____ my two older sisters at the theatre.

g The _____ on Ling's bicycle buckled when he rode into the gutter.

h You _____ very tired this morning.

i My friend and I could not _____ on the best way to make the model.

j Yesterday morning I had to _____ the floors and dust the furniture.

6 Use the clues to find these words that all end in t.
Another clue: The second letter of each word is a, e, i, o or u.

Floating logs tied together	r			t
Money you pay for something you use but don't own	r			t
A noisy disturbance by a lot of people	r			t
To stop working and be quiet	r			t

7   Answer each clue across with a four-letter word. When you have finished, read down the first column to find the name of a fairytale character. One word has been completed.

Clue				
True; not made up or imaginary				
A single thing				
The largest light in the night sky				
The skin or hide of an animal				
Noisy; easily heard; opposite of soft	l	o	u	d
Opposite of odd				
A large bag made of cloth				
The end part of many animals				
A tickling feeling on your skin				
To touch something with your tongue				
Another word for a story				
A piece of canvas on a ship's mast				
A short skirt with a tartan pattern				
A flower; also a part of your eye				
Tidy; in good order				

Build a Word (EA)

8   Write a word that means the remains of a fire.

Add a letter to get a word meaning red spots on your skin.

Add another letter to make a word meaning junk or rubbish.

Challenge words	Find the meaning of these **ee** words and learn how to spell them.

fl**ee**ce	**ee**rie	exc**ee**d	degr**ee**	jambor**ee**
sl**ee**t	fl**ee**t	st**ee**r	r**ee**l	gr**ee**d

ar words

large	party	sugar	march	shark
charge	army	garden	spark	scar

1 **Fill the gaps with words from the list.**

a When my brother turned twenty-one we had a big _____ at the local hall.

b If you put _____ in coffee it will taste sweet.

c An African elephant has _____ ears and a long trunk.

d The spotter plane sounded the alarm when a _____ was seen near a group of swimmers.

e Napoleon's _____ marched through the snow for three months.

f Bill has a small _____ on his stomach from the operation.

g We watched the soldiers _____ during the Anzac parade.

h A small _____ from the burner at the timber mill caused a terrible bushfire.

i At the new coffee shop they _____ three dollars just for a slice of toasted raisin bread.

j Our _____ looked very pretty until the snails ate most of the plants.

2 **Use the clues to complete each word.**

a A white substance used in food and drinks to make them taste sweet ___ ___ ___ ar

b Very big; enormous ___ ar ___ ___

c The mark left on your skin after a wound has healed ___ ___ ar

d A large dangerous fish ___ ___ ar ___

e A large group of soldiers ar ___ ___

Synonyms

3 Choose a word from the box to replace the word in brackets in each of these sentences.
Make sure the word you choose is a synonym for the word in brackets.

cabin	pain	creek	large	store
centre	stomach	away	unusual	sunrise

a Michael was sneezing all day yesterday and today he is (absent) _____

from school.

b The parcel was so (bulky) _____ we couldn't post it in the letter box.

c Julia was in (agony) _____ after falling two metres down the cliff.

d There was a lot of excitement when a platypus was found to be living in a nearby

(stream) _____.

e An insect has three body parts—head, thorax or chest and an (abdomen)

_____.

f The early settlers lived in a small (hut) _____ made from wood.

g I couldn't find what I wanted to buy in the (shop) _____.

h The referee ran to the (middle) _____ of the ground when the game was

about to start.

i The sky was a beautiful colour this morning just after (dawn) _____.

j The platypus is a very (strange) _____ animal.

4 Match these groups of synonyms. There are three words in each group.
Colour each group of words a different colour.

lance	tidy	kill	myth	spear	make
hot	twilight	latest	slaughter	smart	neat
murder	evening	boiling	build	sunset	javelin
new	construct	burning	fable	original	legend

5 This mystery word is an *ar* word found in schools.

co		lar
sim		lar
mar		les
ta		get
p		rty
ha		vest
farm		ard

6 Change *code* to *word* in three moves by changing one letter at a time to form another word.

	c	o	d	e
The middle part of an apple				
Part of the verb 'to wear'				
	w	o	r	d

Build a Word

7 a A large group of soldiers

  b A place where ships stay before going out to sea

  c A hard blackened piece of burnt wood used for drawing

  d Not joined together; divided

  e The part of a garment, such as a shirt or blouse, around the neck

  f Something that is very sweet

  g To look after something, to see that nothing harms it

  h A place, usually out of doors, where people meet to buy and sell food and other things

  i To reach the place you set out for

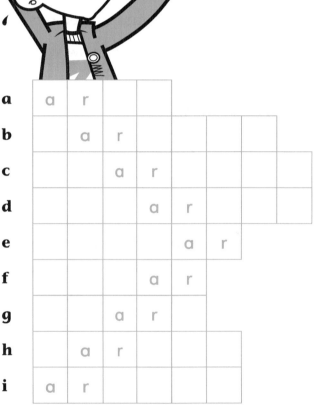

a	a	r				
b		a	r			
c			a	r		
d				a	r	
e					a	r
f				a	r	
g			a	r		
h		a	r			
i	a	r				

Challenge words

Find the meaning of these **ar** words and learn how to spell them.

parched	barb	arch	charm	starch
cargo	garment	remark	similar	harvest

y = 'e' words

hurry	pretty	family	berry	busy
marry	plenty	carry	sorry	only

1 **Complete the sentences with words from the list.**

a Bella was _____ that she had caused the accident.

b There was _____ of food to eat at the barbecue.

c In our _____ there are seven people including Mum and Dad.

d Kim has three sisters but I _____ have one.

e The young woman helped the old lady _____ the heavy parcel.

f The prince thought Snow White was very _____.

g In December the shops are very _____.

h We had to _____ to catch the bus.

i My brother is going to _____ a woman from Adelaide next month.

j I was about to eat the _____ from the tree when my friend said it was poisonous.

2 **Find nine of the list words in this puzzle. Colour in the words as you find them.**

The list word not in the puzzle is

_____.

p	r	e	t	t	y	b	m	s
l	s	o	r	r	y	u	a	b
e	o	n	u	t	h	s	r	e
n	m	l	c	a	j	y	r	r
t	r	y	h	u	r	r	y	r
y	f	a	m	i	l	y	w	y

3 **Write these list words in alphabetical order.**

hurry   family   carry   only   sorry

_____

Now write these list words in alphabetical order.

pretty   berry   busy   plenty

_____

4 Sort out the jumbled letters in this box to find eight of the list words.
One letter will be left over.

| h   yyyyyyy   i   uu |
| aa   rrrrrrr   o   eee |
| c   f   nn   pp   mm |
| ttt   bb   s   lll |

_____   _____

_____   _____

_____   _____

_____   _____

5 Draw a line to match the list word with its definition.

marry   usually people who live together in the same house

pretty   full of activity; plenty to do

berry   to become husband and wife

busy   attractive; pleasant to look at

sorry   a full supply

family   a small, fleshy fruit

plenty   full of regret; wishing you hadn't done something

Word Puzzle

6 Can you solve this puzzle?
To make it easier, you are given three letters of the answer to each clue.

m	a	n					A madman
			a	g	e		A long sea journey
m	a	n					A person who runs a business
				a	g	e	Suitcases and bags
m	a	n					A tropical fruit
				a	g	e	A small town
m	a	n					A large house
				a	g	e	Meat with skin around it

Marvellous Words

7   Can you find these mar words? Use a dictionary if you need to.

    a   A soft, sticky white or pink lolly   mar ___ ___ ___ ___ ___ ___ ___ ___

    b   A round glass ball used in a game   mar ___ ___ ___

    c   An outside shopping centre   mar ___ ___ ___

    d   A dark brownish-red colour   mar ___ ___ ___

    e   The third month of the year   Mar ___ ___

Vertical Words

8   Answer each clue across with a four-letter word. When you have finished, read down the first column to find the name of an Australian state. One word has been done for you.

Clue				
A car you pay to ride in				
Said at the end of a prayer				
A snail-like animal without a shell				
A white liquid which we drink				
An extremely small part of anything	a	t	o	m
Midday; 12 o'clock in the day				
Another word for island				
Tiny insects				

The Australian state is

_____.

Challenge words

In most words ending in **ly**, the **y** has an 'e' sound.
For example: fami**ly**. Find the meaning of these **ly** words and learn how to spell them.

busi**ly**   awkward**ly**   timid**ly**   extreme**ly**   carefu**lly**
fina**lly**   quick**ly**   rough**ly**   easi**ly**   polite**ly**

ck words

packet	pocket	ticket	struck	chicken
bucket	locket	stuck	knock	backwards

1   Use words from the list to complete each sentence.

a   After the heavy rains the tractor was _____ in the mud.

b   The boy fell over when he was trying to run _____.

c   The cow kicked over the _____ of milk.

d   James lost the money because there was a hole in his _____.

e   During the storm the tree was _____ by lightning.

f   Emily had the winning _____ in the raffle.

g   Jo bought the _____ of pumpkin seeds at the nursery.

h   After the football we usually go to the take-away shop and get _____ and chips.

i   Did you hear that _____ at the front door?

j   Yoko lost the _____ she was wearing around her neck.

2   Complete this clueless crossword puzzle by using these ck words.

packet	sock
chicken	suck
truck	clock
lock	pocket
ticket	struck
knock	cricket
bucket	stuck

p	a	c	k	e	t					c	k
c			c	k							
k		c								c	k
		k				c				k	
						k					
							c	k			
							k				c
c				c							k
k			c	k							

Adding 'ing'

Something to remember

When a word ends in a silent **e** we drop the **e** when adding **ing**.
For example: wipe **wiping**   rake **raking**

3   **Add ing to each of these words.**

wave _____   become _____   charge _____

blame _____   curve _____   trace _____

share _____   dine _____   force _____

have _____   wade _____   gaze _____

4   **Using the rule above, change the word in brackets into its correct form in these sentences.**

a   At the end of the war some people were so happy they were

(dance) _____ in the street.

b   I was so angry about the decision the council made I felt like

(write) _____ to the newspaper.

c   The light was quickly (fade) _____ as the sun began to go down.

d   In the 1850s a lot people were (mine) _____ for gold in Victoria.

e   Eleanor was (bake) _____ a cake to take to her grandmother.

f   After we painted the bathroom we began (tile) _____ the shower recess.

g   Stacey was (use) _____ the hairdryer when the power went off.

h   The judge at the show had the job of (taste) _____ all the cakes that had

been entered in the competition.

i   There were hundreds of zebras, antelopes and gazelles (graze) _____

together on the open plains.

j   For our science projects Joel is putting together a PowerPoint presentation on the

computer, but I am (make) _____ a diorama.

5   How many words of three letters or more can you make from the letters in the box? Each
        word must contain the large letter, and each letter can be used only once in each word.

p	a	o
	u	r
s	t	m

_____ _____ _____ _____

_____ _____ _____ _____

_____ _____ _____ _____

_____ _____ _____ _____

6   Add the first letter to make these words complete. Then write the word in full.

___ ream   The thoughts in your mind when you are asleep   _____

___ onvict   Someone who has been sent to prison   _____

___ lizzard   A very windy snowstorm   _____

___ muggle   To bring something secretly into the country   _____

___ hotograph   A picture taken with a camera   _____

___ rchard   A lot of fruit trees growing together   _____

___ essenger   Someone who carries a message   _____

___ orizon   The place where the earth and sky appear to meet   _____

___ ravel   Lots of little pebbles used to make paths   _____

___ able   A short story which is meant to teach us a lesson   _____

___ anoe   A narrow, light boat

7   Make a list of all the ck words you can find. How many end in ck? How many have ck in the
        middle of the word? Did you find any words that begin with ck?

_____ _____ _____ _____ _____

_____ _____ _____ _____ _____

Cross Words (EA)

8   Use the letters below once only to spell words across and down.

s   s   s   l   r   c   d   i   y   y   p   t

| a | | o | | k |

stall	jelly	collect	follow	bullet
shell	jolly	hollow	fellow	gully

1 **Use the words from the list to complete each sentence.**

a The snake was curled up asleep in the _____ log.

b The police officer fired the first _____ into the air as a warning to the runaway prisoner.

c I like to _____ stamps but my sister likes to make models of ships.

d After the race the horse was cooled down and then put in its _____.

e 'You go first and I'll _____ you,' my brother said as we approached the haunted house.

f At the party we had sausage rolls, cakes, ice-cream and _____.

g The heavy rain has washed a lot of mud into the _____.

h Father Christmas is a big, happy person with a _____ laugh.

i Lucy found a very unusual _____ on the beach.

j When my brother turned twenty-one we sang 'For he's a jolly good _____'.

2 **Every time you see a list word, cross it out. You'll be left with a message giving you some information.**

the	stall	female	shell	koala
jelly	has	a	baby	collect
every	year	jolly	when	the
jolly	baby	is	born	hollow
collect	bullet	it	crawls	fellow
into	gully	its	follow	mother's
hollow	pouch	jelly	and	stays
there	stall	for	gully	six
follow	to	collect	seven	bullet
fellow	shell	months	jolly	shell

3 Circle the **ll** in these list words.

follow   gully   collect   bullet   shell

Now write those words in alphabetical order.

_____

4 Draw a line to match the list word with its definition.

stall   a food that sets and stiffens when cool

shell   to go after something; to understand

hollow   a table for goods in a market

follow   a small valley made by running water

bullet   empty inside; a hole or empty place

jelly   a hard outer case or covering

gully   a metal shot used in a gun

5 Which list word goes with these groups of words?

hole	cavity	empty	_____
gather	muster	amass	_____
cheerful	merry	happy	_____
man	friend	mate	_____

What about these ones?

| shop | stable | booth | _____ |
| delay | hesitate | hinder | _____ |

6 Write the list word that is opposite to each of the following.

scatter   _____   solid   _____

unhappy   _____   lead   _____

21

'pro' words

7   Can you find these words that all begin with pro? Use a dictionary to help you.

a   One of the sharp spikes on a fork   pro ___ ___

b   To move about silently and secretly   pro ___ ___

c   To show that what is said is true   pro ___ ___

d   To guard or defend   pro ___ ___ ___ ___

e   A question that is difficult to answer pro ___ ___ ___ ___

f   To speak or sound out words   pro ___ ___ ___ ___ ___ ___

g   To object to something   pro ___ ___ ___ ___

Fits to a T

8   Use the clues to find these words that all end in t.
Another clue: The second letter of each word is a, e, i, o or u.

t			t	A piece of pastry with jam
t			t	To lean to one side
t			t	A shelter you camp in
t			t	A small bunch of grass
t			t	An exam to find out how much you know

l			t	To raise something up
l			t	The opposite side to right
l			t	Coming at the end
l			t	A storeroom under the roof
l			t	Words or numbers in a column

Challenge words

Find the meaning of these ll words and learn how to spell them.

dwell   swell   swill   quell   skull

quill   village   recall   allocate   install

22

Olympic Games words

torch	mascots	medal	events	nations
stadium	ceremony	village	competitors	spectators

archery	swimming	basketball	wrestling	cycling
badminton	pentathlon	hockey	softball	rowing

1   **Unjumble the list words from the first box to complete these sentences.**

a   There are many different types of (snveet) _____ held at the Olympics.

b   The main (stcamso) _____ used when the Olympic Games were held in

Sydney were Syd the platypus, Millie the echidna and Olly the kookaburra.

c   The Olympic (gelivla) _____ is like a small community where athletes

from all nations live together during the Olympic Games.

d   The Olympic (chort) _____ used at the 2004 Olympics in Athens was

designed to look like an olive leaf.

e   Each Olympic Games begins with an opening (moreecny) _____ .

f   There was a loud cheer as the marathon runners entered the

(mutadsi) _____ at the end of the long race.

g   There were many (perscattos) _____ watching the gymnastics final.

h   Everyone clapped when the gold (ladem) _____ was placed around the

athlete's neck.

i   Athletes from many (noitnas) _____ compete at the Olympic Games.

2   **Use the words in the second box to answer these questions.**

a   Which sport is held in the water?   _____

b   Which sport is held on the water?   _____

c   Which sport has a target with a bullseye?   _____

d   Which sport hits a small ball along the ground and into a net?   _____

e   Which sport has a high ring and you throw a ball through it?   _____

f   Which sport is made up of five different events?   _____

Adding 'ing'

Something to remember

When a word has a short vowel followed by only one consonant, the consonant is doubled before we add **ing**. For example:

stop **stopping**   beg **begging**

3 **Add ing to each of these words.**

hop   *hopping*   trip   _____

whip   _____   throb   _____

can   _____   drop   _____

strip   _____   drip   _____

fit   _____   skin   _____

4 **Using the rule above, change the word in brackets so that it fits into the sentence.**

a Chantelle was only (run) _____ slowly when she tripped.

b Paige enjoys playing netball but she much prefers (swim) _____ .

c Carl's family is (travel) _____ around Australia for their holiday.

d When Kevin went ice skating he kept (slip) _____ all over the place!

e During our lunchtime cricket game I was (bat) _____ when the bell rang.

f The small green frog was (hop) _____ from one lily pad to the next.

g Mum is (drop) _____ me off at Rianne's house on Saturday morning

before she goes (shop) _____.

h At school for 'Jump Rope for Heart' we had a (skip) _____ competition.

A Famous Athlete

5 **Each * stands for a letter in the name of a famous Australian athlete. Find the name by writing 13 three-letter words downwards. The first two have been done.**

E	W	S	A	E		A	P	S	T	E	D	A	I
B	E	*	*	*		*	*	*	*	*	*	*	*
B	T	Y	E	E		E	T	Y	E	B	N	T	S

Name the Sport

6   Look at the clues to the seven words below. Find the word that is the answer to each clue. Write the first letter of each word in the square and unjumble these letters to spell the name of a sport.

a   A dried grape used in cakes and puddings   ___ ___ ___ ___ ___ ___

b   The back part of your foot   ___ ___ ___ ___

c   A person who paints pictures   ___ ___ ___ ___ ___ ___

d   A length of time; 365 days   ___ ___ ___ ___

e   To blow up with a loud bang   ___ ___ ___ ___ ___ ___ ___

f   A small furry animal with long ears   ___ ___ ___ ___ ___ ___

g   The middle part of an apple   ___ ___ ___ ___

The sport is _____.

1912 Olympics

7   Answer each clue across with a four-letter word. When you have finished read down the first column to find the name of the city where the 1912 Olympics were held.

A tiny light in the night sky				
Larger than a village but not a city				
To do as you are told				
To heat food before eating				
Two pieces of string tied together	k	n	o	t
A song which praises God				
Not shut				
A young sheep				
A friend; someone you play with				

Revision

1 **Write the correct word.**

beecame	becam	became	_____
prize	prisze	prieze	_____
maer	mayor	maere	_____
cofee	coffe	coffee	_____
knee	nee	knea	_____
suger	shugar	sugar	_____
garden	gardan	guarden	_____
familee	family	famerly	_____
nock	knock	knok	_____
jolly	joly	jollee	_____
sweap	sweep	sweip	_____
medal	medle	meddal	_____
backwoodes	backwards	bakwoods	_____
hurry	hurrie	hury	_____

2 **Write these words into your book and group them into word families.**

rake	hurry	chicken	stuck	knee	between
holiday	display	large	outside	yesterday	packet
prize	collect	chase	busy	awake	hollow
needle	army	mayor	garden	awhile	bucket

3 **Find small words that are in the larger words.**

awake	_____	alive	_____	became	_____
aeroplane	_____	always	_____	fire	_____
holiday	_____	sale	_____	needle	_____
shine	_____	stray	_____	plate	_____
spark	_____	party	_____	white	_____
inside	_____	mayor	_____	display	_____
highway	_____	wheel	_____	army	_____

4 Look at these words. Use them to answer the questions.

tale	jelly	sugar	holiday	yesterday
coffee	wheel	torch	crayon	scar
pocket	white	knock	berry	prize

a Which word is a colour?   _____

b Which word rhymes with porch?   _____

c Which word starts with a silent letter?   _____

d Which word is a great time of the year?   _____

e Which word is a story?   _____

f Which word has two double letters and is a drink?   _____

g Which word means the day before today?   _____

h Which word would you like to eat at a party?   _____

i Which word is very sweet?   _____

j Which word would you find in your jeans?   _____

k Which word would you write or draw with?   _____

l Which word would you like to win?   _____

m Which word is round?   _____

n Which word is found on a bush?   _____

o Which word is left on your body after an operation?   _____

Jumbled Words

5 Unjumble each word. Then write the plural (more than one) for each word.
The first example has been done for you.

a ronyca   crayon   crayons   _____

b eagrdn   _____ _____   **h** yimfal   _____ _____

c kcbuet   _____ _____   **i** eknsa   _____ _____

d oeenaalrp   _____ _____   **j** irepz   _____ _____

e yeecrmno   _____ _____   **k** rebry   _____ _____

f tapry   _____ _____   **l** giavlle   _____ _____

g lltsa   _____   **m** lsidpay   _____ _____

A Giant Word Search

6   How many words can you find in this giant word search? The words go across the page or down the page. Colour in the words as you find them.

A	E	R	O	P	L	A	N	E	M	M	A
A	W	A	K	E	S	L	E	P	O	A	R
S	M	K	B	E	T	W	E	E	N	I	M
C	A	E	M	A	A	A	D	L	L	N	Y
A	F	A	M	I	L	Y	L	E	Y	A	S
R	S	H	E	L	L	S	E	S	E	F	S
B	U	C	K	E	T	W	D	G	A	I	N
A	X	F	A	I	T	H	F	U	L	R	A
C	P	L	A	T	E	I	I	M	C	E	K
K	O	K	U	H	N	T	A	S	A	L	E
W	I	N	V	I	T	E	F	A	I	N	T
A	Y	E	A	G	C	H	I	C	K	E	N
R	Y	E	W	H	E	E	L	E	N	R	S
D	E	O	R	W	F	O	L	L	O	W	I
S	S	F	L	A	R	G	E	Y	C	G	Z
S	T	R	A	Y	F	A	I	L	K	A	E
S	E	E	M	J	R	T	A	L	E	R	V
D	R	A	I	S	E	B	U	S	Y	D	L
E	D	E	P	L	P	R	I	Z	E	E	E
M	A	R	R	Y	Y	I	R	E	P	N	M
O	Y	B	S	H	A	R	K	E	F	S	A
U	A	E	L	R	E	P	L	A	Y	P	Y
T	X	C	S	W	E	E	P	Y	E	R	O
S	L	A	N	E	P	L	S	U	G	A	R
I	C	M	A	C	O	G	U	L	L	Y	X
D	O	E	P	A	C	K	E	T	E	N	I
E	F	I	N	R	K	A	F	R	A	I	D
I	F	N	E	R	E	C	H	A	S	E	P
B	E	R	R	Y	T	S	H	I	N	E	L
J	E	L	L	Y	C	R	A	Y	O	N	A
S	W	A	A	W	H	I	L	E	M	A	N
K	H	G	R	P	A	R	T	Y	Y	G	E
A	I	R	M	A	R	C	H	A	Y	A	Y
T	L	E	E	E	G	L	O	V	E	I	E
E	E	E	M	F	E	L	L	O	W	N	S
A	L	I	V	E	O	P	L	A	I	N	T

ai words

afraid	fail	contain	main	again
raise	faint	faithful	gain	plain

1 Use the clues to complete each word.

a A large flat part of the country   ___ ___ ai ___

b Frightened; full of fear   ___ ___ ___ ai ___

c To hold something inside   ___ ___ ___ ___ ai ___

d Feeling weak and dizzy   ___ ai ___ ___

e To lift up   ___ ai ___ ___

f Most important; chief   ___ ai ___

g Once more   ___ ___ ai ___

h To be unsuccessful   ___ ai ___

i To earn or win   ___ ai ___

j Keeping your promises   ___ ai ___ ___ ___ ___ ___

Word Search

2

a	f	r	a	i	s	e	p
f	a	i	t	h	f	u	l
r	i	p	f	g	a	r	a
a	l	a	g	a	i	n	i
i	o	m	a	i	n	m	n
d	m	a	i	n	t	c	c
c	o	n	t	a	i	n	o

All of the list words are in this puzzle. Can you find them? Colour them as you find them. One list word has been used twice.

Which one is it? _____

3 Circle the ai in these list words.

main   again   raise   plain   faint

Now write these words in alphabetical order.

_____

Compound Words

Something to remember

A **compound word** is made up of two smaller words. For example:

sun + shine = sunshine   rain + bow = rainbow

4   **What are these compound words?**

5   **Use the clues to find two words that, when joined together, make a compound word. The first one has been done for you.**

a   Add a small green vegetable to a male fowl and get a beautiful bird.

pea + cock = peacock

b   Add drops of water that fall out of the clouds to a kind of knot tied in a ribbon and get an arc that you sometimes see in the sky.   _____

c   Add a metal cooking container to something that is sweet and is baked in an oven and get something cooked in a frying pan.   _____

d   Add a motor vehicle for driving to a harbour and get a place where cars are protected from the weather.   _____

e   Add the bottom of anything to a round object used for playing games and get a sport that is very popular in the USA.   _____

f   Add a word that means not heavy to a building we live in and get a tower with a strong light to guide ships at sea in the dark.   _____

6 Complete each sentence with a list word.

a When my work is untidy my teacher tells me to do it _____ .

b The bridesmaid wore a _____ dress without any lace or decorations.

c 'I'll _____ if I see a mouse,' said Tam.

d My little brother always takes his favourite teddy to bed with him because he

is _____ of the dark.

e Does that book _____ all the information you are looking for?

f The mobile crane was used to _____ the car from the bottom of the river.

g My old black labrador is a _____ dog.

h Karen is going for her driver's licence tomorrow so I hope she

doesn't _____ her test.

i On Grand Final day we arrived at the ground early but the _____ match

did not start until two o'clock.

j I hope to _____ another ten points tonight at youth club.

Build a Word (EA)

7

a	a	i						
b		a	i					
c			a	i				
d				a	i			
e					a	i		
f						a	i	
g					a	i		
h					a	i		
i			a	i				
j		a	i					
k	a	i						

a The mixture of gases which we breathe and which surrounds the earth

b A person who makes clothes such as suits, skirts and trousers

c A lot of carriages pulled along a railway by an engine

d Not crooked or curved

e A piece of cloth hanging down to cover a window

f An artificial jet of water

g To give the meaning of something; to make something clear

h To stay behind or to be left

i Metal rings joined together

j The soft covering which grows on your head

k To point a gun or other weapon at the thing you want to hit

| choose | smooth | troop | goose | balloon |
| loose | afternoon | mushroom | roost | bloom |

1 Complete each sentence with a list word.

a We found a _____ growing in the paddock.

b After the party we were each given a piece of birthday cake, some sweets and

a _____ .

c My sister had so many dresses in her wardrobe she didn't know which one

to _____ .

d In the morning it was cloudy but in the _____ the sun was shining.

e At the start of spring the flowers began to _____ .

f The first pair of jeans I tried on were too tight but the next pair were baggy

and _____ .

g At the farm we saw some hens, turkeys, ducks and a _____ .

h Our scout _____ is going on a night hike next week.

i The carpenter used the plane to make the wood _____ .

j The perch or branch where birds sleep at night is called a _____.

2 Use these letters to make as many oo words as you can.

3 Use the clues to complete each word.

a A big bird like a duck with a long neck   ___ oo ___ ___

b At night, birds sleep on a   ___ oo ___ ___

c To take one thing rather than another   ___ ___ oo ___ ___

d A bag filled with air or gas so that it can float

above the ground   ___ ___ ___ ___ oo ___

e The time between midday and sunset   ___ ___ ___ ___ ___ ___ oo ___

4 Use list words to answer these questions.

a Which word rhymes with moose?   _____

b Which word rhymes with boost?   _____

c Which word rhymes with zoom?   _____

d Which word rhymes with loop?   _____

e Which word has the most letters?   _____

f Which word comes first in a dictionary?   _____

g Which word has a double o and a double l?   _____

Fits to a T

5 Use the clues to find these words that all end in t.
Another clue: The second letter of each word is a, e, i, o or u.

A set of clothes	s			t	
Not hard, rough or loud	s			t	
To put things together in groups	s			t	
Told to go somewhere	s			t	
To separate powder from large clumps	s			t	
A white powder used at meal times	s			t	

Words in a Word

6   The middle three letters of each of these five-letter words make a short word. What are the five-letter words?

The short thick finger of your hand		h	u	m	
A number less than ten		e	v	e	
To begin; to move suddenly		t	a	r	
The direction opposite to north		o	u	t	
Where milk, butter and cheese are kept		a	i	r	
A sweet food which is made by bees		o	n	e	

Find the Words

7   Answer each clue across with a four-letter word. When you have finished, read down the first column to find the name of Australia's first Olympic gold medal winner.

A sound that comes back to you	e	c	h	o
To jump headfirst into water				
To shut and open one eye quickly				
Something used to press clothes				
Close to; not far away				

A lot of tiny white bubbles				
Not wanting to work				
A liquid that can burn your skin				
A young cow or bull				
A toy that flies on the end of a string				

Challenge words

Find the meaning of these oo words and learn how to spell them.

brood	boost	stoop	cocoon	droop
ooze	lagoon	booth	spool	noose

ea words

meal	steal	dream	please	easy
real	mean	cheap	leave	wheat

1 **Use the clues to complete each list word.**

a   The thoughts that go on in your mind when you are asleep   ___ ___ ea ___

b   Not difficult; not hard to do or understand   ea ___ ___

c   A kind of grain from which flour is made   ___ ___ ea ___

d   Food eaten at a certain time of the day   ___ ea ___

e   Selfish and unkind   ___ ea ___

f   Not costing much money   ___ ___ ea ___

g   A word you use when you are being polite   ___ ___ ea ___ ___

h   True; not made up or imaginary   ___ ea ___

i   To go away from a place   ___ ea ___ ___

j   To take something that is not yours   ___ ___ ea ___

2 **Every time you see a list word, cross it out. You'll be left with a message giving you some information.**

a	dream	female	wheat	meal
real	koala	leave	is	easy
fully	grown	at	mean	two
years	and	a	dream	steal
steal	male	please	cheap	koala
at	wheat	three	to	mean
easy	four	steal	years	the
word	real	koala	please	comes
cheap	from	an	aboriginal	word
meal	meaning	no	wheat	drink

Plurals

3 Change these words to the plural form. The first one has been done for you.

daisy	daisies	poppy	_____
cry	_____	lady	_____
country	_____	study	_____
hobby	_____	puppy	_____
enemy	_____	city	_____
lolly	_____	army	_____
ferry	_____	fairy	_____
pony	_____	factory	_____
duty	_____	body	_____

4 Using the rule above, change the word in brackets to its plural to fit into the sentences.

a The spray soon killed the (fly) _____ buzzing around in the kitchen.

b Rosanne had ice-cream with her bowl of (strawberry) _____ .

c My dog always (bury) _____ his bones near the elm tree.

d The large city had three (library) _____ .

e The police were kept very busy when there were four (robbery) _____ in one day.

f In our classroom we have four different (dictionary) _____ for reference.

g Nicole borrowed a book from the library called (Mystery) _____ of the World.

h At the training day the (secretary) _____ learnt a new computer program.

5 Write sentences to show what each of these words means.

real _____

reel _____

steal _____

steel _____

cheap _____

cheep _____

Put On Your Thinking Caps! (EA)

6 All of these words start with cap. How many can you find? Use a dictionary to help you.

a A piece of clothing without sleeves that goes over the shoulders   _____

b A person who is in charge of a group of people   _____

c To catch someone and hold them by force   _____

d The greatest amount a container will hold   _____

e The main city of any country; also a large letter of the alphabet   _____

f To jump or leap about happily, usually in a funny way   _____

g To upset and turn upside down, especially a boat   _____

h A tiny container for medicine   _____

Cross Words (EA)

7 Use the letters below once only to spell words across and down.

s   a   c   p   s   b   t   y   n   a   e   p

e | t | U

Challenge words   Find the meaning of these ea words and learn how to spell them.

| plead | least | peat | preach | lead |
| gleam | weave | eager | heave | leader |

oa words

c**oa**st	c**oa**ch	f**oa**m	cl**oa**k
t**oa**st	r**oa**m	f**oa**l	thr**oa**t

1 Use the clues to complete each list word.

a A lot of tiny white bubbles, usually on top of liquid or soapy water ___ oa ___

b Bread which is made brown by heating it ___ oa ___ ___

c The inside of the front of your neck ___ ___ ___ oa ___

d The border of land next to the sea ___ oa ___ ___

e A young horse ___ oa ___

f To wander about ___ oa ___

g A large motor vehicle for long journeys; also someone who
trains sportspeople such as footballers or tennis players ___ oa ___ ___

h A loose garment without sleeves, usually longer than a cape ___ ___ oa ___

2 Put oa in the correct place in each group of letters to make a word.

a bst

b _____

b flt

f _____

c clk

c _____

d tst

t _____

e thrt

t _____

f rst

r _____

g cst

c _____

h fl

f _____

i cch

c _____

j grn

g _____

k rm

r _____

l fm

f _____

3 Circle the oa in these words.

roam   coach   foam   throat   foal   toast

4 Fill the gaps with words from the list.

a The magician wore a top hat and a long black _____ .

b It was early in the morning when the _____ was born.

c Dad burnt the _____ as he was trying to get breakfast.

d My uncle has a holiday house along the _____ .

e The concert was not held because the singer had a sore _____ .

f During the holidays we are going to Wanganui by _____ .

g He started to _____ about the countryside carrying his swag on his shoulder.

h The fire trucks sprayed _____ around the aeroplane that had crash-landed.

5 Can you find all the list words in this puzzle? Colour them in when you find them. There will be seven letters left over. Use the letters to make a word for something found at your school.

i	c	l	o	a	k	c	l
f	o	a	m	r	r	o	b
o	a	t	h	r	o	a	t
a	c	a	t	o	a	s	t
l	h	r	o	a	m	t	y

_____

6 This mystery word is another oa word. You would have one at home.

coa		h
tr		ck
ap		roach
ze		ra
cl		ak
to		st
th		oat
won		erful

7 Write these list words in alphabetical order.

throat   foal   coast   roam

_____

8 How many words of three letters or more can you make from the letters in the box? Each word must contain the large letter, and each letter can be used only once in each word.

	u	l
m		
	d	n
i	e	s

_____   _____   _____

_____   _____   _____

_____   _____   _____

_____   _____   _____

Name the Sport (EA)

9 Look at the clues to the ten words below. Find the word which is the answer to each clue. Write the first letter of each word in the square and unjumble the letters to spell the name of a sport.

a The backbone of a person or animal   __ __ __ __ __

b An aeroplane which carries bombs   __ __ __ __ __ __

c A person who wear gloves and fights   __ __ __ __ __

d A female lion   __ __ __ __ __ __ __

e A scaly reptile with four legs   __ __ __ __ __ __

f A book of maps   __ __ __ __ __

g A poisonous plant like a mushroom   __ __ __ __ __ __ __ __

h The opposite of asleep   __ __ __ __ __

i A large bird of prey   __ __ __ __ __

j The joint in the middle of your leg   __ __ __ __

The sport is _____.

Find the Word (EA)

10 Clues:

• The whole word is a machine that can fly even though it is heavier than air.
• Letters 5, 4, 6, 9 are a long, round, wooden rod.
• Letters 2, 1, 3 are the part of the head through which sounds are heard.

1	2	3	4	5	6	7	8	9

ow words

hollow	fellow	arrow	tomorrow
follow	elbow	narrow	know

1 Use the clues to complete each list word.

a A thin straight stick made of wood with a sharp pointed tip ___ ___ ___ ow

b The joint in the middle of your arm ___ ___ ___ ow

c Having a space or a hole inside ___ ___ ___ ___ ow

d To understand and be sure about something you have

read or seen ___ ___ ow

e To come after someone or something ___ ___ ___ ___ ow

f Slim; not wide; thin ___ ___ ___ ___ ow

g The day after today ___ ___ ___ ___ ___ ___ ow

h A man; a friend or companion ___ ___ ___ ___ ow

2 Complete this crossword using the ow words listed below.

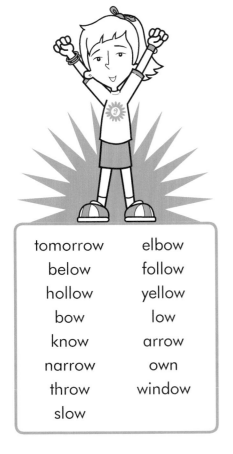

tomorrow   elbow
below   follow
hollow   yellow
bow   low
know   arrow
narrow   own
throw   window
slow

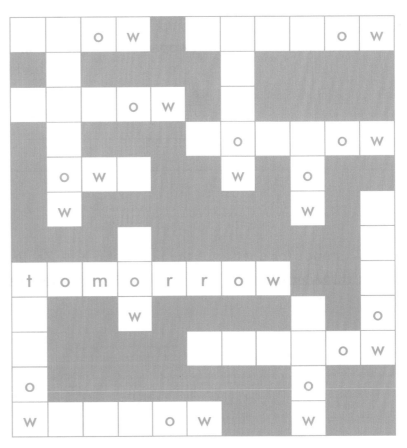

Adding 'ed'

> ### Something to remember
>
> When a word has a short vowel followed by only one consonant, the consonant is doubled before we add **ed**. For example:
>
> drop **dropped**   throb **throbbed**

3   **Add ed to each of these words. The first one has been done for you.**

stop   stopped   hop   _____

trip   _____   whip   _____

beg   _____   strip   _____

can   _____   fit   _____

drip   _____   skin   _____

4   **These pairs of words have become jumbled. Unjumble them and write them out as pairs.**
     The first one has been done for you.

skip	dropped	slipped	ship
bat	shipped	travel	fanned
travelled	skipped	spot	spotted
slip	fan	batted	drop

skip – skipped   _____ _____ _____

_____ _____ _____ _____

Place Names

5   **Each * stands for a letter of the name of a New Zealand city. Find the name by writing**
     eight three-letter words downwards. The first one has been done for you.

R	C	I	S	I	M	O	A
A	*	*	*	*	*	*	*
T	T	E	Y	L	N	E	D

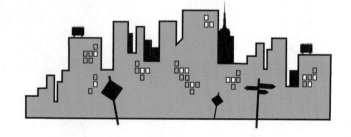

6 Choose the correct word in each sentence.

a When Lee fell over he bruised his (elbow, arrow). _____

b The bridge was so (hollow, narrow) that the cars couldn't pass
each other on it. _____

c Robin Hood fired the (fellow, arrow) through the air. _____

d Do you (elbow, know) whether Swansea is in New South Wales
or Tasmania? _____

e The snake was curled up asleep in the (hollow, follow) log. _____

f You go first and I'll (fellow, follow) you. _____

g (Tomorrow, Elbow) Amber and I are going ice-skating at Skateland. _____

h A (elbow, fellow) my dad knows was given a medal for helping
the police capture an armed robber. _____

Add a Letter

7 Add one letter to the given word to form a new word. Use the clues to help you. The first
one has been done for you.

Given Word	Clue	New Word
pie	A hollow tube	pipe
met	Something we eat	_____
hoe	Where we live	_____
far	A carnival	_____
tie	The coming in of the sea	_____
sea	A fish-eating animal	_____
men	A list of things to eat	_____

Cross Words (EA)

8 Use the letters below once only to spell words across and down.

l l s s t t n i p h w y

i

l

o

or words

porch	order	corner	report	visitor
torch	important	force	doctor	motor

1 **Complete these sentences by using list words.**

   a   The light from the _____ cast strange shadows on the wall.

   b   When my little brother was sick the _____ gave him some large tablets to take.

   c   Last week we had a _____ at our school who came from Japan.

   d   The captain yelled out an _____ to the crew of the ship.

   e   The bus stopped at the _____ of High Street and Valley Road.

   f   For healthy teeth it is _____ that you brush them after every meal.

   g   During the heatwave my brother and I slept on the front _____ .

   h   The model aeroplane was powered by a very small _____ .

   i   Dad was very angry when he read my school _____ .

   j   The _____ of the wind blew the nest out of the tree.

2 **Put or in the correct place in each group of letters to make a word.**

   a   doct   **e**   sne   **i**   mot

       d _____   s _____   m _____

   b   pch   **f**   cner   **j**   recd

       p _____   c _____   r _____

   c   sce   **g**   thn   **k**   sail

       s _____   t _____   s _____

   d   imptant   **h**   fce   **l**   tch

       i _____   f _____   t _____

3 **Underline the or in these words.**

   important   corner   report   visitor   motor   porch

   Now write those words in alphabetical order.

_____

4 Change week to year in three moves by changing one letter at a time to form a new word.

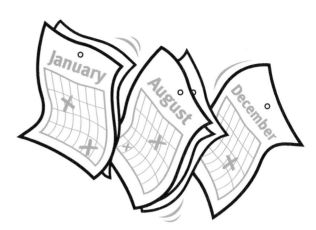

w	e	e	k
				The opposite to strong
				To be dressed in something
y	e	a	r

5 Add the first letter to make these words complete. Then write the whole word.

___ ourney	To travel from one place to another	_____
___ ero	Nothing; the figure 0	_____
___ warm	A large number of bees moving together	_____
___ hantom	A ghost	_____
___ xchange	To give one thing in return for another	_____
___ ider	A drink made from apple juice	_____
___ utumn	The season following summer	_____
___ ennel	A small house for a dog	_____
___ own	A place with many buildings and houses	_____
___ over	To put something on something else	_____

More Compound Words

6 Use the clues to find two words that, when joined together, make another word.

a Add a huge body of water to a relative and get a time of the year. sea + son = season

b Add a piece of wood that stands in the ground to a male person and get a person who delivers letters. _____

c Add the soft edge of the mouth to a long thin piece of wood to get something women use on their faces. _____

d Add something that makes a cool breeze to something that goes around your waist and get a part of a car. _____

e Add something you would write on at Christmas to a long flat piece of wood and get a very thick stiff paper. _____

7 The list word doctor ends in or. Many occupations—or jobs that people do—end in or. Look at the list of occupations in the box below.

doctor	inventor	inspector	councillor	senator
actor	sailor	professor	director	tailor
aviator	conductor	tutor	navigator	editor

Choose three of these words and use them in sentences of your own showing what each one does.

a _____

b _____

c _____

Step Words

8 **a** A lot of fruit trees growing together
   b A large area of land where lots of trees are growing close together
   c To burn slightly; to dry up with heat
   d To write or tell about something that has happened
   e A building where things are made in large quantities, usually by machines
   f A heavy machine with wheels used on a farm
   g To carry something from one place to another (often in a truck or by rail)
   h A moving staircase
   i Someone who teaches or instructs

ou words

flour	cloud	sound	ground	about
loud	thousand	wound	amount	south

1 Choose the correct list word.

a It started to get cold when the sun went behind a (cloud, wound). _____

b The (South, Sound) Island of New Zealand has many lakes and
    waterfalls. _____

c From Perth to Sydney is about four (loud, thousand) kilometres. _____

d There was a (loud, thousand) noise when the petrol tank exploded. _____

e Dad made some delicious pancakes last night using (flour, ground). _____

f Ming is reading a book (loud, about) horses. _____

g The (sound, ground) of the banging door kept me awake last night. _____

h Justin found a large (about, amount) of money hidden in a
    hollow log. _____

i The path (wound, south) through the forest. _____

j We arrived at the football (ground, sound) thirty minutes before the
    match was due to begin. _____

2 Look at these sentences. Underline every word that has ou in it.

a In one hour we will be about a thousand kilometres south of Paris.

b The sound from the football ground was very loud.

c The wheat was ground into flour.

d The track wound through the trees to the picnic ground.

e The silly hound ran around the mound.

47

Homographs

3 **After each sentence write the meaning of the word in green print.**

a When the small boy fell over, a tear began to run down his cheek.

_____

b My teacher said she would tear up my work and make me do it again if it was untidy.

_____

c In just one minute it will be time for lunch.

_____

d The creatures were so minute that you needed a magnifying glass to see them.

_____

e In the sty was a sow with four piglets.

_____

f When autumn comes, farmers sow their crops.

_____

4 **Here are some pairs of homographs. Look at the meaning for each word and then use it in a sentence to show that meaning.**

a wind: the air currents that move around

_____

b wind: to twist and turn

_____

c lead: to show the way

_____

d lead: a soft metal

_____

5 Fit the letters in the boxes to the ou to make as many words as you can.

| c |
| fl |
| m |
| r |
| cl |
| l |
| s |
| sh |
| h |
| f |

ou

| r |
| t |
| th |
| d |
| nd |
| se |
| nt |

_____ _____

_____ _____

_____ _____

_____ _____

_____ _____

_____ _____

_____ _____

_____ _____

_____ _____

_____ _____

6 Write the missing letters to complete these words.

a ___ ound   Anything that can be heard

b ___ ound   Curved like a circle

c ___ ound   A heap of stones or earth

d ___ ___ ound   The earth we walk on

e ___ ___ ound   On all sides

f ___ ound   Not lost

g ___ ound   A hunting dog

h ___ ound   To hit with heavy blows

i ___ ound   Turned and twisted

j ___ ___ ___ ound To astonish or surprise

k ___ ound   To leap forward

Mystery Word (EA)

7 This mystery word is another ou word that causes a lot of problems in some countries, including Australia.

sp		ough
surr		out
tro		und
rou		ble
coug		h
coun		
		ry

Challenge words

Find the meaning of these ou words and learn how to spell them.

| gout | sprout | flounce | flout | drought |
| foul | pounce | astound | trounce | crouch |

Commonly misspelt words 1

answer	many	always	coming	until
guess	enough	bought	except	climbed
laugh	sugar	brought	front	ache

1 **Fill the gaps in these sentences with list words.**

a At the shop I _____ a new computer game.

b Meredith _____ a lizard along to school today.

c Kingsley likes all kinds of chocolate _____ white chocolate, which makes him sick.

d Nick won the competition when we had to _____ how many lollies were in the jar.

e Cameron wanted to buy a bottle of soft drink but didn't have _____ money.

f Maree was in the sick bay because she had a stomach _____ .

g Jasper _____ to the top of the tree.

h 'How _____ stamps do you have in your collection?' asked Peta.

i Sam has three spoons of _____ in her coffee.

j The weather forecast warned that a severe storm is _____ our way.

2 **Use these words in sentences of your own.**

a answer _____

b always _____

c front _____

d until _____

e laugh _____

3 **Write these list words in alphabetical order.**

climbed   sugar   ache   enough   many   brought

_____

4 Draw a line to match the list word with its definition.

answer	to make a noise of amusement
sugar	the foremost part; the opposite to back
guess	a reply
front	continuous pain
laugh	to give an opinion without being sure
ache	a sweet substance made from cane

5 What new words are made when a leaf falls into sand and you cook a tail?

Add a Letter

6 Add one letter to the given word to form a new word. Use the clues to help you. The first one has been done for you.

Given Word	Clue	New Word
hen	Not now	then
bar	A wild animal	_____
ink	To join up	_____
now	To understand	_____
red	Understanding printed words	_____
hit	A clue	_____
ask	Worn on the face	_____
bat	Food used for fishing	_____
tin	Very small	_____
hot	Someone who has guests	_____

Place Name

7 Each * stands for a letter of the name of a district in New Zealand. Find the name by writing ten three-letter words downwards. The first two have been done for you.

A	C	I	A	P	A	E	N	A	B
C	A	*	*	*	*	*	*	*	*
E	T	N	E	N	K	B	T	T	E

Where is 'she'?

8 Use the clues to find these words.

a Large scissors used for cutting sheep's wool   she ___ ___ ___

b The hard covering on a nut   she ___ ___

c Left after a fire   ___ she ___

d Someone who looks after sheep   she ___ ___ ___ ___ ___

e To have thrown liquid around   ___ ___ ___ ___ she ___

f An animal covered with thick wool   she ___ ___

g To have pressed together and squashed   ___ ___ ___ she ___

h A type of US police officer   she ___ ___ ___ ___

i To have gone red in the face   ___ ___ ___ she ___

Name the Sport

9 Look at the clues to the six words below. Find the word which is the answer to each clue. Write the first letter of each word in the square and unjumble those letters to spell the name of a sport.

a A container for carrying water   ___ ___ ___ ___ ___ ___

b Piece of land with water around it   ___ ___ ___ ___ ___ ___

c A covering for the hand   ___ ___ ___ ___ ___

d Slim; thin; not wide   ___ ___ ___ ___ ___ ___

e Very large bird with long legs   ___ ___ ___ ___ ___ ___ ___

f A musical instrument that you hit with wooden hammers   ___ ___ ___ ___ ___ ___ ___ ___ ___

The sport is _____.

1   Write the correct word.

smooth	smoothe	smothe	_____
baloon	balloon	ballon	_____
real	wreal	rill	_____
pleese	plese	please	_____
rome	roam	roame	_____
holow	holloe	hollow	_____
tommorrow	tomorow	tomorrow	_____
motor	moter	mottor	_____
amont	amount	ermount	_____
shugar	suger	sugar	_____
except	exept	eccept	_____
anser	answer	ansar	_____

Jumbled Words

2   Unjumble these words. Then write the plural of each word. The first one has been done for you.

aolblon	balloon	balloons
emal	_____	_____
haocc	_____	_____
oterafnno	_____	_____
ofal	_____	_____
sogoe	_____	_____
ortch	_____	_____
obelw	_____	_____
cluod	_____	_____
osoumhrm	_____	_____

3 Use these words to answer the questions.

mushroom	toast	torch	know	goose
dream	hollow	ache	afternoon	wheat
throat	south	doctor	thousand	answer

a Which word is a part of the day? _____

b Which word is a number? _____

c Which word is a part of your body and rhymes with moat? _____

d Which word is a direction? _____

e Which word shouldn't be confused with a toadstool? _____

f Which word starts with a silent letter? _____

g Which word is a bird found on a farm? _____

h Which word helps you to see in the dark? _____

i Which word is a crop that farmers grow? _____

j Which word follows a question? _____

k Which word rhymes with follow? _____

l Which word happens when you are asleep? _____

m Which word could you have for breakfast? _____

n Which word helps you to get better when you are ill? _____

o Which word is a real pain? _____

4 Write these words into your book and group them into word families.

meal	smooth
coast	please
hollow	ground
real	narrow
cloak	foal
choose	sound
important	order
about	bloom
arrow	elbow
cloud	throat
visitor	

A Giant Crossword

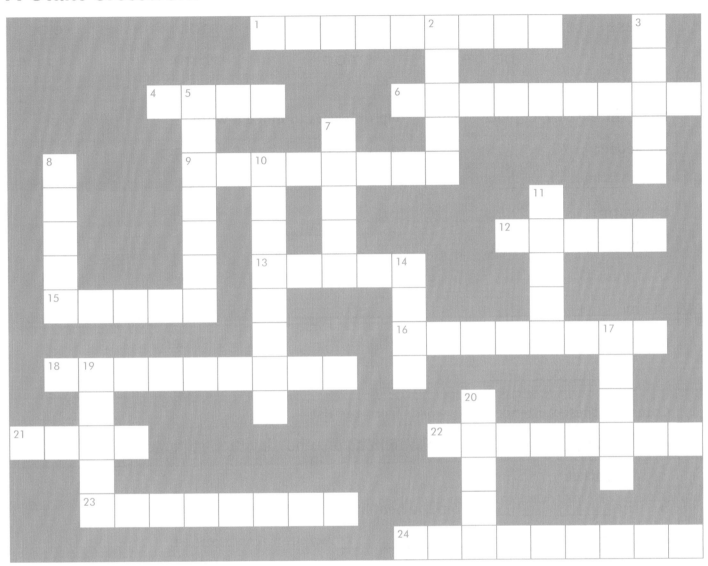

Across

1 Things that cannot be easily explained or understood
4 Something used to press clothes
6 Buildings in which sources of information such as books, newspapers and CDs are kept
9 To get bigger or more in number
12 To make a noise of amusement
13 A book of maps
15 The joint in the middle of your arm
16 A stick of coloured substance used to brighten lips
18 A moving staircase
21 A young horse
22 1000
23 An edible fungus
24 The time between midday and sunset

Down

2 To lift up
3 The thoughts that go on in your mind when you are asleep
5 An arc of different colours that sometimes appears in the sky after rain
7 A precious jewel found inside some oyster shells
8 A large bird of prey with a sharp beak and claws
10 The greatest amount a container will hold
11 Feeling weak and dizzy
14 Fine soil left behind by a river
17 Not costing much money
19 A large number of bees moving together
20 A kind of grain from which flour is made

th words

these	rather	together	mouth	cloth
those	bother	smooth	warmth	clothes

1   Put **th** in the correct place in each group of letters to make a word.

a   togeer

   t _____

b   warm

   w _____

c   moer

   m _____

d   weaer

   w _____

e   smoo

   s _____

f   nor

   n _____

g   feaer

   f _____

h   bo

   b _____

i   cloes

   c _____

j   oer

   o _____

k   tee

   t _____

l   raer

   r _____

2   Complete these sentences with words from the list.

a   I would _____ go swimming on a hot day than go to watch the cricket.

b   The _____ from the heater was making me tired.

c   The cow's legs were tied _____ when it was branded.

d   In the painting of *Mona Lisa*, the woman has a slight grin around her _____ .

e   In winter we wear a lot of _____.

f   It was hard to keep our balance on the _____ ice.

g   Flies _____ cattle and sheep in the summer.

h   The tailor had a large roll of tartan _____ .

i   Would you like _____ lollies or would you rather _____ over there?

3 Complete this crossword using these **th** words.

cloth other
rather bother
health the
mouth smooth
there either
through those
these leather
warmth clothes
together father

4 Add **th** to make these list words.

bo ___ ___ er   toge ___ ___ er   clo ___ ___   smoo ___ ___

___ ___ ese   ra ___ ___ er   warm ___ ___   clo ___ ___ es

5 Use list words to answer these questions.

a Which word has the smaller word get? _____

b Which word has the smaller word arm? _____

c Which word has the smaller word out? _____

d Which word has the smaller word rat? _____

e Which word has the smaller word hose? _____

f Which word has the smaller word both? _____

g Which two words have the smaller word lot? _____ _____

Add a Letter

6 Add one letter to the given word to form a new word. Use the clues to help you.

Given Word	Clue	New Word
bet	Better than all others	best
hoe	To wish something may happen	_____
pad	Given money for goods or work	_____
win	Fast moving air	_____
sat	Furniture for sitting on	_____
arm	A large group of soldiers	_____

'sk' Words (EA)

7 All of these words start with sk. How many can you find? Use a dictionary to help you.

a A metal blade fastened on a shoe so that you can move quickly and smoothly on ice _____

b To slide sideways, as a car sometimes does on wet roads _____

c The outside covering of your body _____

d A very tall building, usually found in cities _____

e A small black animal with white stripes and a bushy tail; it gives out a very bad-smelling liquid when it is in danger _____

f To jump up and down, often on one leg at a time, over a rope _____

g The bones inside your body without the flesh _____

h The bony part of the head _____

i A rough quick drawing or outline _____

j To move quickly over snow on two flat pieces of wood that are fastened to your boots _____

> **Challenge words**
>
> Find the meaning of these **th** words and learn how to spell them.
>
> | | | | | |
> |---|---|---|---|---|
> | thaw | throb | theatre | soothe | depth |
> | froth | breath | breathe | method | bathe |

sh words

shore	shoe	shoulder	finish	splash
share	should	shell	ash	crush

1 Choose the correct list word.

a The footballer hurt his (should, shoulder) when he ran into

the goal post.   _____

b At the quarry a large machine was used to (crush, ash) the

rocks into small stones.   _____

c Yesterday morning a mouse jumped out of my

(shoe, shore) as I was getting ready for school.   _____

d Samantha found a pretty purple (share, shell) at the beach.   _____

e After the fire there was a lot of (crush, ash) blowing in the wind.   _____

f Mark went to play early because he was the first one to

(finish, splash) his work.   _____

g Mum told me to (shoe, share) my lollies.   _____

h Dad made a (splash, shell) as he dived into the pool.   _____

2 Draw a line to match the list word with its definition.

shore	to divide into parts
shoulder	something worn on the foot
ash	to come to an end
shell	to break by pressure
finish	the land at the edge of the sea
shoe	the place where the arms meet the body
crush	the remains of a fire
share	a hard outer case or covering

3 Write these list words in alphabetical order.

should   shell   share   splash

_____

Antonyms

4   Complete these sentences with antonyms for the green words.

   a   Today Shelley is present at school but her sister, Amanda, is _____.

   b   Mr Thompson asked Jack a difficult question and he didn't know

       the _____.

   c   On the way home from the excursion Katie fell asleep in the bus but everyone else was

       _____.

   d   When the police went in the front door, the criminals ran out the _____

       door.

   e   A butterfly is a beautiful creature, but to me a toad is _____.

   f   The lemon tasted bitter but the honey was _____.

   g   Leon lost his new pencil case, but Edan _____ it for him.

   h   Dwayne was really rude to the visitor when he should have been _____.

   i   I was very careful stepping on the rocks crossing the creek, but Josie

       was _____ and fell in the water.

   j   Tan found reading the book easy, but for Laura it was quite _____.

Antonym Noughts and Crosses

5   **Read the word in the middle of each noughts and crosses game. Put a cross on**
    the middle word and on the two other words that are antonyms (opposites).

scream	shout	whisper
yak	yell	cheer
murmur	catch	throw

broad	narrow	thick
yellow	wide	wing
carrot	thin	cloth

tiny	vast	colossal
man	large	woman
giant	nose	small

quit	cease	finish
start	stop	begin
terminate	halt	end

secure	defend	bank
unsafe	safe	dangerous
money	bars	police

damp	dry	soaking
land	wet	drenched
water	arid	moist

Cross Words

6 Use the letters below once only to spell words across and down.

e n n h p p b t s h b e e

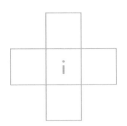 i

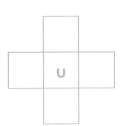 u

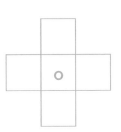 o

Where is 'she'?

7 **a** Something you put on a bed   she ___ ___

    b Plates in which food is served   ___ ___ she ___

    c A place where you are safe from danger   she ___ ___ ___ ___

    d To have hoped for good fortune   ___ ___ she ___

    e To have ended   ___ ___ ___ ___ she ___

    f To have pressed hard against   ___ ___ she ___

    g A small building for tools   she ___

    h A ledge for books   she ___ ___

igh words

high	light	right	bright	fright
night	tonight	midnight	fight	sight

1 **Unjumble the list word in each sentence.**

a Dracula was seen in the street at (giimdnht). _____

b In some countries people drive on the (hirgt) side of the road. _____

c Yesterday my dog had a (tgifh) with a German Shepherd. _____

d The diving tower at the pool looks very (gihh) to me. _____

e An owl can see very well at (hgnit). _____

f When Dad comes home late from work we leave the outside (thgil) on for him. _____

g Louis Braille lost his (gsiht) when he was a young boy. _____

h Jo hid behind the door and gave me a big (thrfig). _____

i (hinoTtg) we are having take-away chicken. _____

j Our neighbours saw a (hgbrit) light in the sky and thought it was a UFO. _____

Block Out

2 **Every time you see a list word cross it out. You'll be left with a message giving you some information.**

the	fright	marathon	right	has
high	become	night	one	of
light	fight	the	most	sight
popular	events	of	tonight	the
bright	Olympic	midnight	high	games
This	light	is	because	of
fright	the	great	bright	stamina
and	right	endurance	that	night
tonight	is	required	of	the
athletes	during	the	midnight	run

3 Circle the **igh** in these list words.

tonight   right   bright   high   night

Now write these words in alphabetical order.

_____

4 Complete this crossword using these **igh** words.

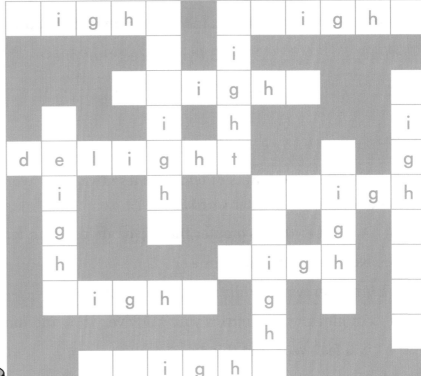

delight   eight
light   high
weigh   sight
tight   knight
slight   fright
tonight   height
weight   eighteen

5 Write the list words that go with these definitions.

a Sudden fear   _____

b Twelve o'clock at night   _____

c A struggle or a combat   _____

d The time of darkness   _____

e Correct or true   _____

f The brightness from the sun or a lamp   _____

6 Add the missing vowels to make these words complete. Write each whole word.

scssrs	A cutting tool	_____
trnp	Large, round root that can be cooked and eaten	_____
trtl	An animal with a shell, like a tortoise	_____
vln	A musical instrument with four strings	_____
nchr	A heavy iron hook attached to a ship by a chain	_____
drm	Images in your mind when you are asleep	_____
msqt	A small flying insect that bites	_____
by	To do as you are told	_____

Words in a Word (EA)

7 The middle three letters of each of these five-letter words make a short word.
What are the five-letter words?

a A number that is greater than five but less than ten

b Not ever; not at any time

c Another word for flat; without any bumps

d An illness which makes your body very hot and makes you feel weak and thirsty

e A bar pushed down at one end so that it lifts something on the other end

f To make a rumbling noise deep down in the throat

g A colour

h To die under water because there is no air to breathe

i To move about silently and secretly

j A lot of people all together in one place

a		e	v	e	
b		e	v	e	
c		e	v	e	
d		e	v	e	
e		e	v	e	
f		r	o	w	
g		r	o	w	
h		r	o	w	
i		r	o	w	
j		r	o	w	

Challenge words

Find the meaning of these **igh** words and learn how to spell them.

th**igh**	sl**eigh**	fr**eigh**t	s**igh**t	al**igh**t
n**eigh**	kn**igh**t	sl**igh**t	pl**igh**t	bl**igh**t

ch words

chair	chance	chase	church	chief
charge	cheap	chalk	change	speech

1 Use the clues to complete each word.

a A building where people go to worship God ch ___ ___ ch

b A soft white stone which can be made into

sticks for writing on the blackboard ch ___ ___ ___

c A piece of furniture to sit on ch ___ ___ ___

d Not costing much money ch ___ ___ ___

e A leader or ruler; the most important ch ___ ___ ___

f To run after; to drive away ch ___ ___ ___

g The act of speaking; also a talk or lecture ___ ___ ___ ___ ch

h Something that happens without being planned ch ___ ___ ___ ___

i To make something different from what it was before ch ___ ___ ___ ___

j The cost of something; also to rush at something ch ___ ___ ___ ___

Word Search

2 Can you find the ten list words in this puzzle? Colour in the words as you find them.

s	i	c	h	i	e	f
p	c	h	a	n	g	e
c	h	a	n	c	e	s
h	a	s	c	h	c	p
e	r	e	h	u	h	e
a	g	m	a	r	a	e
p	e	p	l	c	i	c
s	p	e	k	h	r	h

Plurals

> ## Something to remember
>
> To change words ending in a single **f** or **fe** to the plural, change
> the **f** to **v** and add **es**. For example:
>
> leaf **leaves**   knife **knives**

3 **Change these words to the plural form.**

calf	calves	wolf	_____
loaf	_____	scarf	_____
elf	_____	wife	_____
shelf	_____	half	_____
life	_____	wharf	_____

4 **There are some exceptions to the rule above.**

- For some words that end in **f** we just add **s** to make them plural. For example:
  gulf gulfs   **chief** chiefs

- For some words we can use the rule or just add **s**. For example:
  hoof hoofs or hooves   **wharf** wharfs or wharves

Use these words in sentences of your own.

a chiefs _____

b wharves _____

c hoofs _____

d gulfs _____

e elves _____

5 **Put ch in the correct place in each group of letters to make a word.**

a oose

_____

b pitfork

p _____

c art

_____

d stret

s _____

e sool

s _____

f maine

m _____

g crun

c _____

h ae

a _____

i orid

o _____

6 **Complete each sentence with a word from the list.**

a Eva bought a _____ pair of jeans at the sale.

b Anton started to _____ Rex around the playground.

c When my brother gets home from high school he has to _____ out of his uniform.

d The mayor made a long _____ when the library was opened.

e Lina stood on a _____ when a mouse ran across the floor.

f At _____ on Sunday we sang a new hymn.

g The _____ spoke to the people in his tribe.

h Our teacher drew on the board with _____.

A 'ch' Puzzle

7

Soft side of face below the eyes	c	h				
The land next to the sea					c	h
Shout at someone to do his/her best	c	h				
To hit hard with your fists					c	h
A leader or ruler	c	h				
A bus used for long journeys					c	h
A boy or girl older than a baby	c	h				
To feel something with your fingers					c	h
Game played on black and white board	c	h				
Piece of wood that makes fire					c	h
A map, usually of the sea	c	h				
To set something up, like a tent					c	h

Challenge words   Find the meaning of these **ch** words and learn how to spell them.

chafe	chariot	cheque	chute	choir
ache	orchestra	orchid	stomach	machine

le words

ankle	cattle	middle	battle	saddle
bottle	apple	candle	simple	needle

1 Complete these sentences with words from the list.

a When our electricity supply was cut off we had to light a _____.

b Heidi sprained her _____ when she tried to jump over the log.

c The stockman rounded up the stray _____.

d I usually find maths hard but today's test was _____.

e The wild horse began to buck when we tried to put a _____ on it.

f Ashley bought a _____ of soft drink at the milk bar.

g The workers painted the line down the _____ of the road.

h William Tell fired an arrow through an _____ on his son's head.

i The soldiers prayed before they went into _____.

2 Use the letters in this box to make seven list words. One letter is left over. Write ten words that begin with the extra letter.

aaaa	ss	mmm	b	ddddd	tt
llllll	k	ppp	nn	ii	eeeeeeeee

_____   _____   _____   _____   _____

_____   _____   _____   _____   _____

_____   _____   _____   _____   _____

_____   _____

3 Use the clues to find the list word.

My first letter is in soil but not in boil.

My second letter is in bag and also in hat.

My third is in old but not in loan.

My fourth is in diet and also in wood.

My fifth is in lake but not in bake.

My sixth is in fare and also in pen.

What am I? _____

4 What list words, when put in the spaces, make three-letter words reading across?

e		b
b		y
a		e
s		y
s		y
n		t

u		e
a		r
i		p
a		e
f		y
t		n

i		e
t		n
a		t
o		d
s		y
p		n

a		e
b		y
a		e
s		y
a		e
h		n

e		t
o		e
s		y
e		f
g		m

c		p
a		e
a		t
i		l
p		a

5 Write all the list words that

a start with letters a–h

_____

_____

_____

_____

_____

_____

b start with letters i–o

_____

_____

c start with letters p–z

_____

_____

d contain a double letter

_____

_____

_____

_____

_____

_____

Fits to a T

6 Use the clues to complete these words that all end in t.
Another clue: The second letter of each word is a, e, i, o or u.

f			t	A tightly closed hand
f			t	A strong building to keep enemies out
f			t	A thick woollen material
f			t	A part of your body
f			t	Very quick; opposite to slow
f			t	Something that is true
f			t	More than one foot

7 How many words of three letters or more can you make from the letters in the box? Each word must contain the large letter, and each letter can be used only once in each word.

b	r	y
	e	a
i	n	m

_____ _____ _____

_____ _____ _____

_____ _____ _____

_____ _____

Place Name

8 Each * stands for a letter of the name of an Australian city. Find the name by writing eight three-letter words downwards. The first two have been done for you.

P	O	P	O	C	P	O	E
A	D	*	*	*	*	*	*
T	D	N	D	T	N	D	L

Find the Word

9 Clues:

- The whole word is a musical instrument
  played with the hand or shaken to give a tinkling sound.
- Letters 9, 2, 3, 10 are the word by which a person is known.
- Letters 1, 5, 6, 7 mean a journey to various places for pleasure.

1	2	3	4	5	6	7	8	9	10

Challenge words

Find the meaning of these **le** words and learn how to spell them.

muscle	idle	buckle	stifle	particle
tremble	bristle	mingle	article	circle

oil	soil	foil	point	join
spoil	boil	voice	noise	poison

1 Use the clues to complete each list word.

a Something swallowed or injected that can make you very

ill or even kill you ___ oi ___ ___ ___

b Loose earth; also to make something dirty ___ oi ___

c A thick greasy liquid which can come from animals or plants,

or from under the ground oi ___

d A sound which is sometimes very loud ___ oi ___ ___

e To damage something or make it of no use ___ ___ oi ___

f To put together or fasten ___ oi ___

g The sound that comes from people's mouths when they speak

or sing ___ oi ___ ___

h To make water so hot that it bubbles and makes steam ___ oi ___

i The sharp end of something, like a pin or a pencil ___ oi ___ ___

j To prevent from succeeding ___ oi ___

2 Use the letters to make as many oi words as you can.

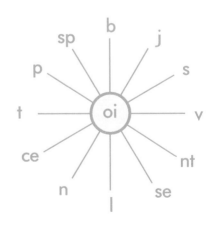

_____ _____ _____ _____ _____

_____ _____ _____ _____ _____

Homonyms Revisited

3   **Use a dictionary to find the meanings of the homonyms in green print.**

boil   **a**   Damian went to the doctor because he had a very painful boil under

his arm. _____

   b   To cook potatoes you need to boil them for twenty minutes.

_____

soil   **c**   Amber raked the soil before she planted the seeds.

_____

   d   Young babies often soil their clothes when they are feeding.

_____

foil   **e**   The prisoner had a good plan so no-one could foil his attempt to escape.

_____

   f   After Sue baked the apple pie she covered it with foil.

_____

   g   The champion Olympic fencer had a very light foil.

_____

point   **h**   The point of the needle was very sharp.

_____

   i   We won the match by one point.

_____

   j   There's no point in wasting time.

_____

   k   For our holiday we went to Point Lonsdale.

_____

4 Put *oi* in the correct place in each group of letters to make a word.

a vce

v ___ ___ ___ ___

b cn

c ___ ___ ___

c spl

s ___ ___ ___ ___

d jnt

j ___ ___ ___ ___

e nse

n ___ ___ ___ ___

f pnt

p ___ ___ ___ ___

g jn

j ___ ___ ___

h tlet

t ___ ___ ___ ___ ___

i pson

p ___ ___ ___ ___ ___

j sl

s ___ ___ ___

k avd

a ___ ___ ___ ___

l nsy

n ___ ___ ___ ___

5 Unjumble the list word in each sentence.

a The rabbit died because it ate the carrot that had been dipped in (noopis).

_____

b When Leanne had the flu she lost her (vcioe).

_____

c The mechanic put a litre of (lio) in our car.

_____

d The (eonis) from the explosion shattered the windows in nearby shops.

_____

e When Marie leaves school she wants to (nioj) the navy.

_____

f Worms are very good for the (soli).

_____

g The (nipot) on my pencil keeps breaking.

_____

h In the old days before electricity my grandma had to (lobi) water in a large pot over a fire.

_____

i If you write too quickly you might (liosp) your work.

_____

Find the Word (EA)

6 Clues:
- The whole word is a musical instrument with a number of narrow bars of different lengths.
- Letters 6, 7, 3, 9 are a hollow space.
- Letters 4, 1, 9, 8 mean more than one ox.

1	2	3	4	5	6	7	8	9

knee	knife	knew	lamb	write
know	knot	knock	thumb	wrote

1 **Complete these sentences with words from the list.**

a Graham broke his _____ when he tried to catch the cricket ball.

b There was a loud _____ on the door.

c At Scouts we learnt how to tie a reef _____ and to make a stretcher.

d Last night I _____ to my pen-friend who lives in Canada.

e The footballer was on crutches after the operation on his _____.

f Fiona likes to _____ stories about horses.

g I didn't _____ my nine times table so my teacher gave me some homework to do.

h The _____ was bleating because it couldn't find its mother.

i Elaine cut her hand on a very sharp _____.

j I _____ the answer to the question so I won a prize.

Block Out

2 **Every time you see a list word cross it out. You'll be left with a message giving you some information.**

lamb	knock	whales	live	thumb
in	the	sea.	write	wrote
knee	they	know	belong	knot
to	the	same	family	knew
as	knife	cats	giraffes	knock
elephants	knee	dogs	and	lamb
knee	even	humans	knee	thumb
they	write	know	are	write
knot	all	knew	lamb	know
knife	knock	mammals	knot	wrote

3 Write the list words to match these definitions.

a The short thick finger _____

b The place on a piece of rope where it has been tied _____

c A young sheep _____

d The middle joint of the leg _____

e A sharp blade on a handle _____

f To strike with a hard blow _____

4 Write these list words in alphabetical order.

knee   know   knife   knot   knew   knock

_____

5 Use the clues to find these words that all contain s and w.

a To grow larger   SW ___ ___ ___

b Fast; quick; rapid   SW ___ ___ ___

c Dry, stiff yellow stalks   S ___ ___ ___ W

d A soft sticky white or pink lolly   ___ ___ ___ S ___ ___ ___ ___ ___ ___ W

e Food between two pieces of bread   S ___ ___ ___ W ___ ___ ___

f A caterpillar that spins silk threads   S ___ ___ ___ W ___ ___ ___

g The opposite of deep   S ___ ___ ___ ___ ___ W

h A seat hanging from ropes or chains   SW ___ ___ ___

i Long sharp weapon used for fighting   SW ___ ___ ___

j To join cloth with needle and thread   S ___ W

Word Puzzle

6   How many words of three letters or more can you make from the letters
in the box? Each word must contain the large letter and each letter can
be used only once in each word. Write the answers in your book.

	r	m
C	s	a
e	t	o

More Words with Silent Letters

7   Use these words in sentences of your own.

crumb   _____

bomb   _____

climb   _____

comb   _____

gnat   _____

sign   _____

knit   _____

knob   _____

wrong   _____

Name the Sport (EA)

8   Look at the clues to the eight words below. Find the word that is the answer to each clue.
Write the first letter of each word in the square and unjumble these letters to spell the
name of a sport.

a   The thin part of your arm that joins your hand   __ __ __ __ __

b   A sugar coating for cakes   __ __ __ __ __

c   A sudden brief fall of rain   __ __ __ __ __ __

d   An animal that swings in trees   __ __ __ __ __ __

e   To make a noise like a pig   __ __ __ __ __

f   The hard part at the end of a finger   __ __ __ __

g   Heavy bicycle with a motor   __ __ __ __ __ __ __ __ __

h   A hut made of blocks of hard snow   __ __ __ __ __

The sport is _____.

Australian and New Zealand cities

Melbourne	Wellington	Brisbane	Darwin	Perth
Sydney	Auckland	Dunedin	Invercargill	Geelong
Adelaide	Christchurch	Canberra	Hobart	Palmerston

1 Complete this table using list words.

Australian cities	New Zealand cities

2 Write these list words in alphabetical order.

Melbourne   Sydney   Adelaide   Darwin   Hobart

_____

Now write these list words in alphabetical order.

Wellington   Auckland   Palmerston   Dunedin   Invercargill

_____

3 This mystery word is a city in New Zealand.

tra		e
b		ndle
wi		ter
forg		t
gar		en
fr		nge
to		gue

The mystery word is _____.

Plurals

4   **Change these words to the plural form. The first one has been done for you.**

crash	crashes	bus	_____
fox	_____	splash	_____
address	_____	circus	_____
buzz	_____	witch	_____
princess	_____	gas	_____
flash	_____	bush	_____
kiss	_____	guess	_____
lunch	_____	dress	_____
speech	_____	stitch	_____

5   **Match the words with their plurals. Colour each pair you find a different colour.**

bunch	ash	boxes	benches	punches
beach	dishes	box	beaches	hutches
bunches	patch	bench	ashes	punch
dish	stitches	patches	stitch	hutch

6   **Write any smaller words found in these list words. For example:**
Newcastle = new, cast, castle

a   Christchurch _____   **e**   Palmerston _____

b   Brisbane _____   **f**   Geelong _____

c   Adelaide _____   **g**   Dunedin _____

d   Wellington _____   **h**   Invercargill _____

7 How many syllables are in each of these list words? Write your answer in the box beside each word.

Geelong ☐   Christchurch ☐   Wellington ☐

Perth ☐   Palmerston ☐   Hobart ☐

Dunedin ☐   Invercargill ☐   Sydney ☐

Name the City

8 Use the clues to find the name of each of these cities.

a Originally called Bearbrass, this city was later named after Lord Melbourne, a British Prime Minister. _____

b Australia's oldest and largest city, this city was named after Lord Sydney, a British politician. _____

c This city is the capital of New Zealand. _____

d Founded in 1866, this city was named after Lord Palmerston, a British Prime Minister.

_____

e John Stokes named this city after the famous scientist and naturalist, Charles Darwin.

_____

f This city was named after Lord Hobart, a British politician. _____

g This city is the capital of Queensland and was named after Sir Thomas Brisbane, a Governor of New South Wales. _____

Place Name (EA)

9 Each * stands for a letter of the name of an Australian town. Find the name by writing ten three-letter words downwards. The first two have been done for you.

E	C	P	S	T	O		S	P	A	A
B	R	*	*	*	*		*	*	*	*
B	Y	T	Y	A	E		E	T	L	E

The city is _____.

1 **Choose the correct word.**

smoth	smooth	smoothe	_____
shu	shooe	shoe	_____
krush	crush	cruish	_____
mouth	mooth	mouf	_____
hi	high	highe	_____
midnite	midknight	midnight	_____
chase	chace	chaise	_____
chief	cheif	chieve	_____
kattle	cattle	cattel	_____
poison	poisun	posion	_____
knok	knock	nock	_____
wrote	rote	wrot	_____

Jumbled Words

2 **Unjumble these words. Then write the plural of each word. The first one has been done for you.**

uomht	mouth	mouths
oshe	_____	_____
sah	_____	_____
ghlit	_____	_____
hccruh	_____	_____
richa	_____	_____
elttob	_____	_____
iobl	_____	_____
balm	_____	_____
nefki	_____	_____
hmtub	_____	_____

3 Use these words to answer the questions.

mouth	midnight	boil	ankle	chalk
shell	write	clothes	saddle	right
chair	apple	spoil	thumb	lamb

a Which word is a part of the foot? _____

b Which word has five letters and rhymes with foil? _____

c Which word is a piece of furniture you can sit on? _____

d Which two words sound the same? _____ _____

e Which word could be found at the beach or on the back of a snail? _____

f Which word is a young farm animal? _____

g Which word would you wear? _____

h Which word has a double letter and is something you would eat? _____

i Which word is found on your face? _____

j Which word rhymes with pork? _____

k Which word would you put on a horse? _____

l Which word is the best time of the day for ghosts? _____

m Which word is on your hand? _____

n Which word has four letters and would be very hot? _____

4 Find a smaller word in each of these words.

these _____	rather _____	together _____	finish _____
share _____	shoe _____	shoulder _____	sight _____
fright _____	chair _____	cheap _____	tonight _____
cattle _____	spoil _____	know _____	needle _____
knew _____	simple _____	Invercargill _____	saddle _____
Brisbane _____	midnight _____	voice _____	battle _____
point _____	poison _____	candle _____	splash _____

A Giant Word Search

5 How many words can you find in this giant word search? The words go across the page or down the page. Colour in the words as you find them.

```
J A C O S T U M E O I L
S L A M B U H I G H I R
P A T C H N N E C A S H
O N C K N E E C H A I R
I T H U M B E A A S G C
L H A W S A D D L E H R
O E N A H T L O K V T U
T S K T E S E T P E T S
O E L C L O T H E S S H
G O E H L I B O I L C J
E K N E W L Z S T O R N
T W O M K C H E A P A I
H U G E N W R O T E T G
E S P E E C H M A T C H
R A T H E R B R I G H T
H E K I T C H E N V O M
B E C L O T H K N O T U
O V K F I G H T F O I L
T O N I G H T S H A R E
H I O R U L E M F U S E
E C W R I T E O T O C M
R E A G O O D O S B H I
C R R S M O U T H E I D
A A M U S E S H O R E N
F N T S P L J I E I F I
I S H O U L D S L G P G
N P G F E J O I N H O H
I L I G H T A M O T I T
S A C H E A P P I M N F
H S G O I N P L S I T L
P H C A N D L E E D F U
K C H A R G E A M D R T
N L U P O I S O N L I E
I L R C H A N G E E G M
F Y C B U T C H E R H Y
E S H O U L D E R W T I
```

tch words

ca**tch**	pa**tch**	ki**tch**en	wa**tch**
ma**tch**	scra**tch**	bu**tch**er	swi**tch**

1 Use the clues to complete each list word.

a A person who cuts up meat and sells it   ___ ___ tch ___ ___

b A small piece of cloth used to cover a hole in clothes   ___ ___ tch

c This is used to turn on a light   ___ ___ ___ tch

d A room where cooking is done   ___ ___ tch ___ ___

e A small thin piece of wood or cardboard with a tip that makes fire   ___ ___ tch

f To look closely; also a small clock you wear on your wrist   ___ ___ tch

g A mark made with something sharp   ___ ___ ___ ___ tch

h To get hold of something   ___ ___ tch

2 Write these list words in alphabetical order.

patch   kitchen   butcher   watch   catch

What Am I?

3 Use the clues to find the list word.

My first letter is in brain and also in best.

My second is in cup but not in clip.

My third is in tall and also in after.

My fourth is in chair but not in hair.

My fifth is in hate but not in plate.

My sixth is in even and also in petrol.

My seventh is in rabbit but not in habit.

What am I? _____

Adding 'ful'

Something to remember

One l from **full** is dropped when this word is added to the end of another word. For example:
'full of wonder' becomes **wonderful**

4 Add **ful** to these words. The first one has been done for you.

hope	hopeful	harm	_____
peace	_____	doubt	_____
power	_____	grace	_____
care	_____	pain	_____
use	_____	help	_____
thank	_____	colour	_____
cheer	_____	joy	_____

5 Wonderful means full of wonder. Using the rule above, find the answers to the clues below. Remember each one will end in ful.

a full of joy   _____   **g** full of tact   _____

b full of care   _____   **h** full of shame   _____

c full of success   _____   **i** full of pain   _____

d full of power   _____   **j** full of truth   _____

e full of dread   _____   **k** full of help   _____

f full of fright   _____   **l** full of doubt   _____

6 Use the letters in the box to make six list words. One letter will be left over.
Write ten words that begin with the extra letter.

aaaa	ii	cccccccc	r	b
ttttt	m	hhhhhh	k	n
ww	ss	e		

My ten extra words are

_____   _____

_____   _____

_____   _____

My six list words are

_____   _____

_____   _____   _____   _____   _____

_____   _____   _____   _____   _____

7 What list words when put in the spaces make three-letter words reading across?

e		b
r		b
a		e
i		e
t		e
p		w
c		y

s		y
p		e
s		y
a		e
s		e
s		e
e		d

a		s
i		e
t		y
s		w
a		e
a		e
t		e

u		e
e		e
p		e
a		e
a		e
s		e

a		e
m		t
a		e
i		e
t		e

i		e
r		m
s		y
a		e
s		e

Find the Word

8 Clues:
- The whole word means a high-ranking naval officer.
- Letters 7, 4, 6, 5 mean a person who does not tell the truth.
- Letters 3, 1, 4, 2 mean a female servant.

1	2	3	4	5	6	7

Birds

9 Fit the words in Column A into the correct spaces in Column B to make different birds.

Column A	Column B
bin	peli ___ ___ ___
in	mag ___ ___ ___
can	___ ___ ___ on
bat	flam ___ ___ go
her	ro ___ ___ ___
pie	al ___ ___ ___ ross

voice	sentence	force	fence	twice
once	pencil	circus	chance	peace

1 **Unjumble the list words in these sentences.**

a Toni and I tried to get a job at the (uriccs) selling popcorn. _____

b Many fairy tales begin with '(nOec) upon a time ...' _____

c Justin ripped his trousers trying to get through the

barbed-wire (cnefe). _____

d The artist made a quick sketch of the sailing ship with a (cnepil). _____

e After the war there were 30 years of (capee). _____

f We had to write each list word in a (cteeesnn) of our own. _____

g The actor had a deep, husky (eciov). _____

h The (eofrc) of the wind blew the tiles off the roof of the church. _____

i Mr Lee has been fined (cwtie) for speeding. _____

j We found a lovely, quiet picnic spot just by (haccne). _____

2 **Can you find the ten list words in this puzzle? Colour in the words as you find them. Two have been used twice. What are they?**

_____   _____

p	e	n	c	i	l	f	o	x
e	j	v	o	i	c	e	e	p
a	s	e	n	t	e	n	c	e
c	i	r	c	u	s	c	t	n
e	a	j	e	a	n	e	w	c
f	o	r	c	e	o	n	i	i
n	t	w	i	c	e	n	c	l
j	a	c	h	a	n	c	e	c

3 What list words, when put in the spaces, make three-letter words reading across?

u	e
p	n
o	e
s	y
h	n
a	t
a	e
p	t

a	e
p	n
a	t
a	t
b	s
u	e

e	e
p	d
p	t
i	e
b	t

o	f
y	s
e	d
i	e
l	t

w	n
o	e
a	e
l	g

s	y
o	e
l	p
i	e
t	n

Missing O

4 Put o back into into the correct places in these words.

smth	Without any bumps; the opposite of rough	_____
pisn	Something which causes illness or death when taken	_____
pppy	A plant, usually with bright red flowers	_____
beetrt	A dark red vegetable	_____
acrn	The nut or seed that grows on an oak tree	_____
buy	Something floating on the water but anchored to the sea bed	_____
xylphne	A musical instrument	_____
wdwrk	Another word for carpentry	_____
vercat	A coat worn over all your other clothes	_____
enrmus	Very large; huge	_____
babn	A large monkey with a short tail	_____
bacn	Pig meat that has been dried and salted	_____
chse	To take one thing rather than another	_____
dur	A very strong smell	_____

5   Which list words match these definitions?

a   A pointed tool, without ink, used for writing or drawing   _____

b   A travelling show of animals, acrobats, etc.   _____

c   Freedom from war   _____

d   The sound given out through the mouth   _____

e   Two times   _____

f   One time   _____

g   Boards, posts, wire, etc. used to enclose a property   _____

h   Strength or power   _____

Find the Word

6   Clues:

- The whole word is a publication which comes out every week or month.
- Letters 1, 2, 7, 8 mean the long hair some animals (such as horses) have on their neck.
- Letters 3, 4, 5, 8 mean to look at something steadily; to stare.

1	2	3	4	5	6	7	8

Countries

7   Fit the words in Column A into the correct spaces in Column B to make countries of the world.

Column A	Column B
ran	En __ __ __ __ __
Fin	__ __ __ ada
gland	K __ __ ea
mark	F __ __ __ ce
Can	Holl __ __ __
lay	__ __ __ land
or	Den __ __ __ __
It	Ma __ __ __ sia
and	__ __ aly

soft g words

giant	hedge	large	giraffe	change
edge	ledge	magic	germ	village

1 **Use the clues to complete each list word.**

   a A very tiny bit of animal or plant life that you can see only

   under a microscope; some can cause disease   g ___ ___ ___

   b Houses and buildings all together, like a town but smaller   ___ ___ ___ ___ ___ g ___

   c The end of something like a table or a shelf; also the cutting

   side of a knife   ___ ___ g ___

   d A very big strong person, usually in fairy stories   g ___ ___ ___ ___

   e To make something different from what it was before   ___ ___ ___ ___ g ___

   f Very big   ___ ___ ___ g ___

   g A tall animal with a very long neck   g ___ ___ ___ ___ ___ ___

   h A narrow flat shelf   ___ ___ ___ g ___

   i An imaginary power that makes wonderful things happen

   that seem impossible, like changing a frog into a prince   ___ ___ g ___ ___

   j Lots of bushes growing close together in a line, like a fence   ___ ___ ___ g ___

More Soft g Words

2 **Six of these words contain a soft g—ones that have a 'j' sound. Can you find them?**

gentle	greet	ginger	game	gander	gypsy
goat	general	gym	gum	guard	generous

   _____   _____   _____

   _____   _____   _____

3 **Write the soft g words in alphabetical order.**

   village   hedge   magic   edge   giraffe

   _____

Contractions

4   Choose the contractions from the box to match each group of words below. Write the contraction next to the long form of the word.

a   she is   _____   **f**   are not   _____

b   do not   _____   **g**   we will   _____

c   I am   _____   **h**   it is   _____

d   is not   _____   **i**   we are   _____

e   cannot   _____   **j**   you are   _____

I'm	isn't
you're	aren't
she's	can't
we're	don't
it's	we'll

5   Use these contractions in sentences of your own.

a   wouldn't _____

b   he's   _____

c   didn't   _____

d   here's   _____

e   I've   _____

Fits to a T

6   Use the clues to find these words that all end in t. The second letter in each word is a, e, i, o or u.

To make something hot	h			t
To give pain	h			t
To stop	h			t
To chase after something you want to catch	h			t
Person who has others as guests	h			t

7 Add the first letter to make these words complete. Then write the word in full.

___ corn	The nut or seed that grows on an oak tree	_____
___ hin	The part of your face under your mouth	_____
___ ough	The loud noise you make when you have a sore throat	_____
___ ough	The opposite of smooth	_____
___ dult	A person who is fully grown up	_____
___ ighty	Another word for powerful or strong	_____
___ ress	To push against or push down	_____
___ ircle	A completely round ring	_____
___ hale	The largest animal found in the sea	_____
___ oad	An animal that looks like a frog	_____
___ mall	Another word for little	_____
___ ketch	A rough, quick drawing	_____

Name the Sport (EA)

8 Look at the clues to the nine words below. Find the word which is the answer to each clue. Write the first letter of each word in the square and unjumble these letters to spell the name of a sport.

a A piece of thick cloth that you dry
   yourself with   ___ ___ ___ ___ ___

b A bright flash of light in a stormy sky   ___ ___ ___ ___ ___ ___ ___ ___ ___

c A type of animal with six legs   ___ ___ ___ ___ ___ ___

d A person who acts in a film   ___ ___ ___ ___ ___

e A room in a school   ___ ___ ___ ___ ___ ___ ___ ___ ___

f To feel something with your fingers   ___ ___ ___ ___ ___

g The opposite to crooked or curved   ___ ___ ___ ___ ___ ___ ___ ___

h Reason for not doing something   ___ ___ ___ ___ ___ ___

i An aircraft that can go straight   ___ ___ ___ ___ ___ ___ ___ ___ ___ ___
   up or down

   The sport is _____.

ore words

tore	core	more	sore	shore
store	score	pores	wore	explore

1 **Unjumble the list word in each sentence.**

   a I will (tosre) the wine in the cellar.   _____

   b In the sports pages of the newspaper the (ocser) from

   the football match was not correct.   _____

   c May I have some (erom) chocolate please?   _____

   d When my uncle has an apple he eats the (ocre) as well.   _____

   e I (erwo) my gum boots to school today because it is so wet.   _____

   f Pimples occur when the (speor) of the skin become clogged.   _____

   g The shipwrecked sailor waded along the (horse).   _____

   h Karen (rote) her jumper on the wire fence.   _____

   i My knee is still very (rose) from when I fell over last week.   _____

   j The curious kitten left his basket to (rxlepoe) the backyard.   _____

2 **Add these letters to ore to make as many words as you can.**

b	
c	
m	
sn	
sh	
st	
sc	
w	

ore → _____
_____
_____
_____
_____
_____
_____
_____

3 Use the letters in the box to make seven list words. One letter will be left over. Write ten words that begin with the extra letter.

ssss	t	rrrrrrr	eeeeeeee
cc	l	x	pp
h	ooooooo		w

The seven list words are

_____ _____

_____ _____

_____ _____

_____

My ten extra words are

_____ _____

_____ _____

_____ _____

_____ _____

_____ _____

4 Find the list words that go with these definitions.

a The land at the edge of the sea _____

b Past tense of wear _____

c Greater in quantity or number _____

d To keep count; also a group of twenty _____

e Past tense of tear _____

f A supply of things for future use _____

g To search or examine _____

h Tender or painful _____

i The middle part of an apple _____

j Small openings in the skin _____

5 How many words of three letters or more can you make from the letters in the box? Each word must contain the large letter, and each letter can be used only once in each word.

t	a	p
	s	r
o	g	e

_____ _____ _____ _____

_____ _____ _____ _____

_____ _____ _____ _____

_____ _____ _____ _____

_____ _____ _____ _____

Find the Word

6   Answer each clue across with a four-letter word. When you have finished read down the first column to find the name of something you probably love to eat.

Winged animal with feathers	b	i	r	d
Floating logs tied together				
A solemn promise				
The sea when still and without waves				
A walking stick				
Not round but egg-shaped				
To like someone very much				
Lazy; doing nothing				

Build a Word

7   Write down a word that means a metal.

Add a letter to get a word meaning ripped.

Add a letter to get a word meaning a shop.

Anagrams

8   Change the order of the letters to work out the new words.

a   Change spot into a word meaning to send a letter.   _____

b   Change rat into a word meaning painting, drawing, pottery, etc.   _____

c   Change mane into a word meaning not kind.   _____

d   Change ring into a word meaning a smile.   _____

e   Change arm into a word meaning a male sheep.   _____

f   Change lips into a word meaning to fall over.   _____

g   Change time into a word meaning one thing only from a list, etc.   _____

h   Change shore into a word meaning a type of animal.   _____

ie words

pie	tie	lied	cried	died
lie	die	dried	tried	fried

1 Can you find eight of the list words in this puzzle? Colour in the words as you find them. Which two words have not been used? Make another ie word from the five letters in the puzzle that are left over.

d	r	i	e	d	e	t
i	p	i	e	i	t	i
e	f	r	i	e	d	e
d	c	r	i	e	d	h
t	r	i	e	d	i	f

- The words not used are

  _____ and _____

- Another five-letter ie word is _____

2 Choose the correct list word to complete the sentence.

a   Felicity (fried, cried) _____ when her cat was hit by the car.

b   After body surfing in the ocean Grant (dried, died) _____ himself with the beach towel.

c   'I hope you will never (lie, tie) _____ to me,' said Mum.

d   I usually take my lunch to school, but yesterday I bought a

(fried, pie) _____ from the canteen.

e   On Anzac Day and Remembrance Day we think of the soldiers who

(died, die) _____ during the wars.

f   Before I started school I already knew how to (lie, tie) _____ my shoelaces.

g   Homophones are words that have the same sound, but different meanings and

spellings, like dye and (pie, die) _____.

h   When the principal spoke to Brett he told the truth, but Malcolm

(lied, tried) _____ .

i   I like my eggs (dried, fried) _____.

j   The maths test was hard but I (cried, tried) _____ as hard as I could.

ie or ei?

3   **Put ie into these words, then use them in sentences.**

   a   th ___ ___ f   _____

   b   f ___ ___ rce   _____

   c   br ___ ___ f   _____

4   **Put ei into these words, then use them in sentences.**

   a   rec ___ ___ ve   _____

   b   v ___ ___ l   _____

   c   r ___ ___ gn   _____

5   **Add ie or ei to these words. Write the whole word.**

   c ___ ___ ling   _____   br ___ ___ f   _____

   w ___ ___ ght   _____   fr ___ ___ nd   _____

   th ___ ___ f   _____   p ___ ___ ce   _____

   th ___ ___ r   _____   f ___ ___ ld   _____

   dr ___ ___ d   _____   bel ___ ___ ve   _____

Looking Back

6   **Complete these sentences.**

   a   Today I laugh.   Yesterday I laughed.

   b   Today I sing.   Yesterday I _____

   c   Today I drink.   Yesterday I _____

   d   Today I cough.   Yesterday I _____

   e   Today I teach.   Yesterday I _____

   f   Today I fly.   Yesterday I _____

Write It Backwards

7   Find the answer to the first clue in each set. Then write that word backwards and you will
    have the answer to the next clue.

   a   Something that you put rubbish in   ___ ___ ___

   b   The point of a pen   ___ ___ ___

   c   A short, quick sleep   ___ ___ ___

   d   Used for cooking food in   ___ ___ ___

   e   Dried wheat stalks   ___ ___ ___ ___ ___

   f   Small hard growths on the skin   ___ ___ ___ ___ ___

   g   The rise and fall of the sea   ___ ___ ___ ___

   h   Prepare for publication   ___ ___ ___ ___

   i   A big hole in the ground   ___ ___ ___

   j   The end of a stick   ___ ___ ___

   k   Something you get water from   ___ ___ ___

   l   To touch lightly   ___ ___ ___

Words in a Word

8   Each of these six-letter words ends with a three-letter word. Use the clues to find the word.

a	A kind of dancing which tells a story in movement				l	e	t
b	A place where motor cars are kept or repaired				a	g	e
c	A person who shoots at a target with a bow and arrow				h	e	r
d	A piece of land where flowers, fruit or vegetables are grown				d	e	n

Challenge words   Find the meaning of these **ie** words and learn how to spell them.

| achievement | relieve | grieve | wield | applied |
| frieze | belief | besiege | relied | replied |

er words

person	timber	shelter	master	newspaper
serve	number	later	teacher	offer

1 Fill the gaps with words from the list.

a In the _____ we read about the earthquake near Los Angeles.

b Alex was the last _____ to get off the bus.

c The _____ after ninety-nine is one hundred.

d If you work in a shop you have to _____ customers.

e The servant opened the door for the _____.

f We are going on a picnic _____ in the day.

g We did not get wet waiting for the bus because we were under the bus _____ .

h The frame of the house was made of _____.

i I'll _____ you twenty swap cards for your badge.

j Our _____ never growls.

2 Can you find the ten list words in this puzzle? Colour in the words as you find them.

c	t	e	s	t	m	r	o	t
n	e	w	s	p	a	p	e	r
a	a	p	e	r	s	o	n	t
i	c	c	l	a	t	e	r	i
l	h	o	f	f	e	r	t	m
s	e	r	v	e	r	u	n	b
c	r	n	u	m	b	e	r	e
a	r	s	h	e	l	t	e	r

3 Eight of the list words end in er. Make a list in your book of all the words you can find that end in er. Can you think of any words that begin with er?

Step Words

4	**a**	Mistake; something that has been done incorrectly	e	r							
	b	The outside measurement of an area		e	r						
	c	A bright green precious stone			e	r					
	d	Up-to-date; not old-fashioned				e	r				
	e	A girl who has the same parents as you					e	r			
	f	Not as old as someone else						e	r		
	g	A person who speaks to others, usually in a church							e	r	
	h	A printed daily paper that tells you about things that have happened recently								e	r

Add a Letter

5   Add one letter to the given word to form a new word. Use the clues to help you.

Given Word	Clue	New Word
oar	To fly high	soar
pot	A poetry writer	_____
even	Something that happens	_____
down	To die underwater	_____
soar	To do with the sun	_____
sore	Number of goals in a game	_____
came	A desert animal	_____

Find the Word

6   Clues:

- The whole word is a musical play for children, usually based on a fairy tale.
- Letters 6, 7, 3, 4 are a place where coins are made.
- Letters 1, 5, 9, 4 are someone who writes poetry.

1	2	3	4	5	6	7	8	9

Bird Watching (EA)

7   Place the words in Column A in the places in Column B to make the names of different types of birds. Write each bird's name in full.

Column A	Column B
wall	___ ___ ___ ch
fin	c ___ ___ ___
star	tur ___ ___ ___
row	s ___ ___ ___ ___ ow
bin	___ ___ ___ ___ ling
key	ro ___ ___ ___

_____

_____

_____

_____

_____

_____

Name the Sport (EA)

8   Look at the clues to the six words below. Find the word that is the answer to each clue. Write the first letter of each word in the square and unjumble these letters to spell the name of a sport.

a   A piece of money made of metal   ___ ___ ___ ___

b   A small house for a dog   ___ ___ ___ ___ ___ ___

c   Another word for good-looking   ___ ___ ___ ___ ___ ___ ___ ___

d   A small boat with sails   ___ ___ ___ ___ ___

e   Very bad; wicked   ___ ___ ___ ___

f   A shellfish that sometimes has a pearl in it   ___ ___ ___ ___ ___ ___

The sport is _____.

Challenge words

Find the meaning of these **er** words and learn how to spell them.

lantern	permanent	flounder	diameter	temper
perfect	perhaps	quarter	foreigner	proper

tt words

cotton	button	bottle	cattle	kitten
bottom	battle	matter	settle	little

1   Use the clues to complete each list word.

   a   A young cat   ___ ___ tt ___ ___

   b   One word for cows, bulls and oxen   ___ ___ tt ___ ___

   c   A fight   ___ ___ tt ___ ___

   d   Thread or cloth made from a part of a plant   ___ ___ tt ___ ___

   e   A container, usually made of glass which has a narrow neck

          and is used to hold liquids   ___ ___ tt ___ ___

   f   The lowest part of anything   ___ ___ tt ___ ___

   g   Not big; the same as small   ___ ___ tt ___ ___

   h   To agree upon something, such as how much to sell a car for   ___ ___ tt ___ ___

   i   A round fastening on clothes   ___ ___ tt ___ ___

Block Out

2   Every time you see a list word, cross it out. You'll be left with a message giving you
    some information.

the	cotton	kangaroo	bottom	button
is	battle	a	bottle	marsupial
matter	which	means	that	matter
the	kitten	mother	button	carries
cattle	her	young	in	cattle
a	cotton	pouch	a	little
young	little	kangaroo	battle	is
settle	called	a	joey	settle
kangaroos	usually	move	bottle	around
in	bottom	groups	called	mobs

Plurals

3 **Change these words to plurals.**

potato _____   cargo _____

tomato _____   volcano _____

echo _____   mosquito _____

dingo _____   domino _____

4 **Change these words to plurals.**

silo _____   banjo _____

radio _____   solo _____

Eskimo _____   folio _____

studio _____   merino _____

5 **Use these words in sentences of your own.**

a mangoes _____

b echoes _____

c kangaroos _____

d photos _____

'tt' Search

6 **Look through books, magazines, newspapers, etc. How many words can you find that contain tt? Make a list of them.**

_____ _____ _____ _____ _____

_____ _____ _____ _____ _____

_____ _____ _____ _____ _____

Countries

7 Fit the words in Column A into the correct spaces in Column B to make countries of the world.

Column A	Column B
ice	__ __ __ __ __ a
us	An __ __ __ ctica
way	Yu __ __ slavia
land	__ __ __ land
Chin	A __ __ tralia
tar	Nor __ __ __
tin	Tur __ __ __
go	Argen __ __ __ a
key	Po __ __

Find the Word

8 Clues:
- The whole word is a long-distance foot race of 42 kilometres.
- Letters 1, 2, 5 mean a material that covers the floor.
- Letters 5, 3, 2, 1 are a passenger vehicle like a bus that runs on rails.

1	2	3	4	5	6	7	8

Words in a Word

9 The middle three letters of each of these five-letter words make a short word. What are the five-letter words?

a	A thick slice of meat		t	e	a	
b	To wrinkle your forehead when you are angry or not pleased		r	o	w	
c	To frighten or alarm		c	a	r	
d	To walk in step; also a month of the year		a	r	c	
e	The hard white parts of our body which are joined together to make the skeleton		o	n	e	
f	A little seat with no back or arms		t	o	o	
g	A long flat piece of wood		o	a	r	
h	A very strong metal made from iron		t	e	e	
i	Strings used to tie up shoes		a	c	e	

any	again	doctor	choose	used
among	empty	beginning	answer	sure
break	front	chose	knew	anchor

1 Write the list word to match the clue.

a Containing nothing; the opposite to full _____

b The start or commencement _____

c A reply or solution to a problem _____

d A ship's mooring hook _____

e A person who treats illnesses or injuries _____

f Certain or confident _____

g To shatter; also to tame _____

h The first or most forward part _____

i Surrounded by; amidst _____

j Once more _____

2 Choose **means to select or to pick out.** Chose **is the past tense of** choose. **Place** choose **or** chose **into these sentences.**

a Today I am going shopping to _____ a dress for my brother's wedding.

b The dress I _____ was pink with a large bow at the back.

c When Mum said we could have anything for tea I _____ pizza but Danni _____ fish and chips.

d 'I don't know which one to _____,' said Lisa.

3 Write these letters in alphabetical order.

k   u   s   e   c   _____

Now write these words in alphabetical order.

used   chose   empty   knew   sure

_____

Now write these words in alphabetical order. (You may need to look at the second or third letters.)

any   among   answer   anchor   again

_____

Build a Word

4   **a**   Write down the name of an animal like a large mouse.

Add a letter to get a word meaning to evaluate or grade.

Add a letter to get a word meaning a large wooden box.

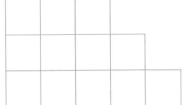

b   Write down a word meaning to succeed; to be victorious.

Add a letter to get one of two children born at the same time.

Add a letter to get a word meaning very strong string.

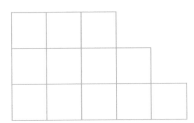

Double Letters

5   Put in the correct pair of double letters.

| nn | ll | tt | ss |

ga ___ ___ op   bo ___ ___ om   ki ___ ___ en   ke ___ ___ el   ca ___ ___ ot

le ___ ___ on   me ___ ___ age   tu ___ ___ el   i ___ ___ ness   blo ___ ___ om

a ___ ___ ract   a ___ ___ end   bu ___ ___ on   co ___ ___ ect   acro ___ ___

fo ___ ___ ow   te ___ ___ is   co ___ ___ on   fla ___ ___ el   sci ___ ___ ors

Word Chain

6   Change **pig** to **sty** in five moves by changing one letter at a time to form another word.

p	i	g	
			Large, great
			A sack or pouch
			An inward curve or the shore line
			To speak or state
s	t	y	

Fits to a T

7   Use the clues to complete these words that all end in t. Another clue: the second letter of each word is a, e, i, o or u.

Something that is given as a present	g			t
Tidy; in good order	n			t
A short skirt with a tartan pattern	k			t
The one after	n			t
An animal a bit like a sheep	g			t
To move forwards in jerky movements	j			t
A small animal like a lizard	n			t
Say something to make people laugh	j			t
A bird's home where eggs are laid	n			t

T-sers

8   Unjumble the letters in capitals.

a   Add t to hole and get a place where you can buy alcohol or rent a room. _____

b   Add t to race and get a large box used for packing fruit, vegetables, etc. _____

c   Add t to sore and get a place where you can buy things. _____

d   Add t to chap and get a small piece of material used to mend things. _____

e   Add t to horn and get a direction. _____

f   Add t to fig and get something which is given as a present. _____

g   Add t to seal and get a kind of stone used for roofs. _____

h   Add t to die and get the coming in and going out of the sea. _____

i   Add t to spire and get a man in charge of a church. _____

j   Add t to age and get a door in a fence or wall. _____

1 **Choose the correct words.**

anka	anchor	ankor	_____
onse	once	wonce	_____
jerm	geerm	germ	_____
explore	exploor	explor	_____
tried	treid	tride	_____
villaj	villiage	village	_____
master	marster	marstir	_____
cach	catch	catche	_____
tried	treid	tryed	_____
botle	bottel	bottle	_____
twice	twise	twiece	_____
jiant	giant	gaint	_____
core	coor	caw	_____

Jumbled Words

2 **Unjumble these words. Then write the plural of each word. The first once has been done for you.**

ecipnl	pencil	pencils
cnfee	_____	_____
aefrigf	_____	_____
roste	_____	_____
henktic	_____	_____
ided	_____	_____
ttamer	_____	_____
wsnepprae	_____	_____
merg	_____	_____
wtach	_____	_____
ttbuon	_____	_____
ktneti	_____	_____

3 Look at these words. Use them to answer each question.

circus	switch	peace	newspaper	giraffe
germ	bottle	match	answer	large
core	butcher	cattle	button	pie

a This word could cause you to become ill. _____

b This word is something you read. _____

c This word sounds the same as piece but has a different meaning. _____

d This word rhymes with battle and means a group of cows, bulls or oxen. _____

e This word means very big. _____

f This word means to change something. _____

g This word has a double letter and is an unusual African animal. _____

h This word is a person who prepares meat for sale. _____

i This word gives us a lot of fun and comes from an old Latin word meaning circle or ring. _____

j You can use this word to light a fire. _____

k This word is a food that is made of meat in a pastry case. _____

l This word means the middle of something. _____

m This word means a round fastening on clothes. _____

n This word means to reply to a question. _____

o This word is made from sand. _____

4 Write these words into your book and group them into word families.

magic	patch	hedge	explore	button	sore
force	score	switch	shore	died	tried
store	ledge	offer	germ	later	kitten
fence	kitchen	twice	die	village	catch
pie	person	peace	serve	fried	settle

A Giant Crossword

Across

1 Reason for not doing something
5 A bright flash of light in a stormy sky
7 A word that has the same sound as another but a different meaning and spelling
8 A half of a half
9 A kind of small arrow
11 Full of power
13 Something floating on the water but anchored to the sea bed
15 Activities you do in your spare time
18 A high-ranking naval officer
20 Very large, huge
22 A mark made with something sharp
24 A ship's mooring hook
25 A narrow, flat shelf
26 The very best that something can be

Down

2 Full of colour
3 A girl who has the same parents as you
4 Lots of bushes growing together in a line, like a fence
6 A piece of land where flowers, fruit or vegetables are grown
10 The opposite of smooth
12 Many fairy tales begin with this word
14 A large monkey with a short tail
16 A round fastening on clothes
17 A rough, quick drawing
19 The largest animal found in the sea
21 To do with the sun
23 The middle part of an apple

List and Challenge words

a–e
rake
awake
snake
sale
tale
lane
became
plate
skate
chase
plane
aeroplane

ay
holiday
always
display
replay
stray
spray
major
crayon
highway
yesterday

ar
large
charge
party
army
sugar
garden
march
spark
shark

scar
parched
barb
arch
charm
starch
cargo
garment
remark
similar
harvest

i–e
prize
size
while
awhile
alive
fire
shine
white
invite
inside
outside
beside

ee
needle
knee
between
wheel
speech
coffee
agree
steep
sweep

seem
fleece
eerie
exceed
degree
jamboree
sleet
fleet
steer
reel
greed

y = 'e'
hurry
marry
pretty
plenty
family
carry
berry
sorry
busy
only
busily
awkwardly
timidly
extremely
carefully
finally
quickly
roughly
easily
politely

ck
packet
bucket
pocket
locket
ticket
stuck
struck
knock
chicken
backwards

ll
shell
jelly
jolly
collect
hollow
follow
fellow
bullet
gully
dwell
swell
swill
quell
skull
quill
village
recall
allocate
stall
install

ea
meal
real
steal
mean
dream
cheap
please
leave
easy
wheat
plead
gleam
least
weave
peat
eager
preach
heave
lead
leader

ai
afraid
raise
fail
faint
contain
faithful
main
gain
again
plain

oo
loose
smooth
afternoon
troop
mushroom
goose
roost
balloon
bloom
choose
brood
boost
stoop
cocoon
droop
ooze
lagoon
booth
spool
noose

oa
coast
toast
coach
roam
foam
foal
cloak
throat

ow
hollow
follow
fellow
elbow
arrow
narrow
tomorrow
know

or
porch
torch
order
important
corner
force
report
doctor
visitor
motor

ou
flour
loud
cloud
thousand
sound
wound
ground
amount
about
south
gout
sprout
flounce
flout
drought
foul

pounce
astound
trounce
crouch

tch
catch
match
patch
scratch
kitchen
butcher
watch
switch
latch
clutch
stretch
satchel
wretched
retch
snatch
ratchet
hutch
dispatch

er
person
serve
timber
number
shelter
later
master
teacher
newspaper
offer
lantern
permanent
flounder
diameter

temper
perfect
perhaps
quarter
proper
foreigner

sh
shore
share
shoe
should
shoulder
shell
finish
ash
splash
crush

th
these
those
rather
bother
together
smooth
mouth
warmth
cloth
clothes
thaw
throb
theatre
soothe
depth
froth
breath
breathe
method
bathe

igh
high
light
right
bright
fright
night
tonight
midnight
fight
sight
thigh
sleigh
freight
alight
neigh
knight
slight
plight
blight

ch
chair
charge
chance
cheap
chase
chalk
church
change
chief
speech
chafe
chariot
cheque
chute
choir
ache
orchestra

orchid
stomach
machine

soft c
voice
once
sentence
pencil
force
circus
fence
chance
twice
peace

Olympic Games
torch
stadium
mascots
ceremony
medal
village
events
competitors
nations
spectators
archery
badminton
swimming
pentathlon
basketball
hockey
wrestling
softball
cycling
rowing
aquatics

gymnastics
Paralympics
pavilion
Olympian
athletics
medley
venue
equestrian
synchronised

le
ankle
battle
cattle
apple
middle
candle
simple
saddle
needle
muscle
idle
buckle
stifle
particle
tremble
bristle
mingle
article
circle
bottle

soft g

giant
edge
hedge
ledge
large
magic
giraffe
germ
change
village

Australian and New Zealand cities

Melbourne
Sydney
Adelaide
Wellington
Auckland
Christchurch
Brisbane
Dunedin
Canberra
Darwin
Invercargill
Hobart
Perth
Geelong
Palmerston

oi

oil
spoil
soil
boil
foil
voice
point
noise
join
poison

ore

tore
store
core
score
more
pores
wore
shore
sore
explore

tt

cotton
bottom
button
battle
bottle
matter
cattle
settle
kitten
little

Silent letters

knee
know
knife
knot
knew
knock
lamb
thumb
write
wrote

ie

pie
lie
tie
die
lied
dried
cried
tried
died
fried
achievement
frieze
relieve
grieve
belief
besiege
wield
relied
applied
replied

Commonly misspelt words

answer
guess
laugh
many
enough
sugar
always
bought
brought
coming
except
front
until
climbed
ache
any
among
break
again
empty
front
doctor
beginning
chose
choose
answer
knew
used
sure
anchor

Word extensions from list words

agree
agreeable
agreeably
agreed
agreeing
agreement

ankle
anklet

apple
apple cart
apple pie

army
armies
arms

ash
ashen
ashes

awake
awaken
awakening
awaking
awoke
awoken

balloon
ballooned
ballooning
balloonist

battle
battled
battlefield
battleground
battler
battleship
battling

berry
berries
berrying

beside
besides

bloom
bloomed
bloomer
blooming

boil
boiled
boiler
boiling

bottle
bottlebrush
bottled
bottleneck
bottling

bottom
bottomless

bright
brighter
brighten

bucket
bucketful

bullet
bulletproof

busy
busied
busier
busiest
busily

button
buttoned
buttoning

candle
candlelight
candlestick

carry
carried
carrier
carries
carrying

catch
catches
catching
catchment
catchy
caught

chance
chanced
chancier
chanciest
chancing
chancy

charge
chargeable
charged
charger
charging

chase
chased
chaser
chasing

cheap
cheaper
cheapish
cheaply
cheapness

choose
choosing
choosy
chose
chosen

church
churches
churchyard

cloak
cloakroom

cloth
cloths

clothes
clothed
clothing

cloud
clouded
cloudier
cloudiest
cloudy

coast
coastal
coasted
coaster
coastguard
coasting
coastline

collect
collected
collectible
collecting
collection
collector

contain
contained
container
containing
containment

cotton
cotton wool

crush
crushed
crushing

die
died
dies
dying

display
displayed
displaying

doctor
doctorate
doctored

dream
dreamed
dreamer
dreaming
dreamless
dreamt
dreamy

easy
easier
easiest

edge
edged
edgily
edging
edgy

elbow
elbowed
elbowing

explore
exploration
exploratory
explored
explorer
exploring

fail
failed
failing
failure

faithful
faithfully

family
families

fence
fenced
fencer
fencing

finish
finished
finishes
finishing

fire
fiery
fire brigade
fired
fire engine
fire escape
fire
extinguisher
firefly
fireplace
firework
firing

flour
floury

foam
foamed
foaming

foil
foiled
foiling

follow
followed
follower
following

force
forced
forceful
forcefully
forcefulness
forcible
forcibly
forcing

foul
fouled
foully
foulness

fried
fries
fryer
frying

gain
gained
gainful
gainfully
gaining

garden
gardened
gardener
gardening

germ
germicidal
germicide

goose
geese
goosebumps
gosling

ground
grounded
grounding
groundless

gully
gullies

hedge
hedged
hedgehog
hedger
hedging

high
height
higher
highest
highlight

hurry
hurried
hurrying

knee
kneed
kneecap

knife
knifed
knifing
knives

knock
knocked
knocker
knocking
knock-kneed
knock out

knot
knotted
knotty

know
knew
know-how
knowing
known

large
largely
larger
largest

leave
leaver
leaving
left

lie
liar
lied
lying

light
lighted
lighter
lightest
lighthouse
lighting
lightly
lightness
lights
lightweight
lit

little
littler
littlest

loose
loosed
loosely
looseness
looser

loud
louder
loudest
loudly
loud-mouth
loudness
loudspeaker

magic
magical
magically
magician

main
mainly

match
matched
matches
matching
matchless

matter
mattered
mattering

meal
mealtime

mean
meaning
meaningful
meaningless
meant

middle
middleweight
middling

more
moreover

motor
motorboat
motorcross
motorcycle
motored
motoring
motorise
motorist
motorway

mushroom
mushroomed
mushrooming

narrow
narrowed
narrower
narrowest
narrowly
narrowness

needle
needling

noise
noiseless
noisier
noisiest
noisily
noisy

number
numbered
numbering

offer
offered
offering

oil
oiled
oiling
oily

order
ordered
ordering
orderliness

outside
outsider

party
parties

patch
patched
patches
patching
patchwork
patchy

peace
peaceful
peacefully

pencil
penciled
penciling

person
personable
personage
personal
personalities
personality
personally

please
pleased
pleasing

plenty
plentiful
plentifully

point
pointed
pointer
pointing
pointless

poison
poisoned
poisoner
poisoning
poisonous

porch
porches

pretty
prettier
prettiest
prettily
prettiness

prize
prized
prizing

raise
raised
raising

rake
raked
raking
rakish

real
realism
realist
realistic
realistically
realities
reality
really

replay
replayed
replaying

report
reportable
reported
reporting

right
right angle
righted
righteous
rightfully

roam
roamed
roaming

roost
rooster

saddle
saddled
saddler
saddlery
saddling

sale
saleability
saleable
salesperson

scar
scarred
scarring

score
scored
scorer
scoring

scratch
scratched
scratches
scratching

sentence
sentenced
sentencing

serve
served
server
serving

settle
settled
settlement
settler
settling

share
shared
shareholder
sharing

shell
shelled
shelling

shelter
sheltered
shelterer
sheltering

shoe
shod
shoelace
shoestring

should
shouldn't

shoulder
shouldered
shouldering

sight
sighted
sighting
sightless
sight lines
sightseeing
sightseer

simple
simpler
simplest
simplicity
simplification
simplified
simplify
simplistic
simply

size
sizeable
sizeably

skate
skated
skater
skating

smooth
smoothed
smoothest
smoothing

soil
soiled
soiling

sore
sorely
sorer
sorest

sorry
sorrier
sorriest

sound
sounded
soundest
sounding
soundless
soundproof

south
southerly
southern
southerner
southward
sou'wester

spark
sparked
sparking
sparkle
sparkled
sparkler
sparkling

speech
speeches
speechify
speechless

spoil
spoiled
spoiling
spoilt

spray
sprayed
sprayer
spraying

stall
stalled
stalling

steal
stealing
stole
stolen

steep
steeped
steeper
steepest
steeping

store
storage
stored
storekeeper
storing

stray
strayed
straying

sugar
sugared
sugary

sweep
sweeper
sweeping
swept

thousand
thousandth

thumb
thumbed
thumbing

tie
tied
tying

timber
timbered

toast
toasted
toaster
toasting

torch
torches

tore
torn

tried
trier

troop
trooped
trooper
trooping

visitor
visiting
visited

voice
voiced
voicing

watch
watched
watches
watchful
watchfulness
watching

weather
weathered
weathering

wheel
wheelbarrow
wheeled
wheeling
wheelwright

wound
wounded
wounding

write
writer
writing
written
wrote

Progress record sheet

Unit	Date completed	Comments: teacher, parents or student
Unit 1 **a–e** and **i–e** words		
Unit 2 **ay** words		
Unit 3 **ee** words		
Unit 4 **ar** words		
Unit 5 **y = 'e'** words		
Unit 6 **ck** words		
Unit 7 **ll** words		
Unit 8 Olympic Games words		
Unit 9 Revision		
Unit 10 **ai** words		
Unit 11 **oo** words		
Unit 12 **ea** words		
Unit 13 **oa** words		
Unit 14 **ow** words		
Unit 15 **or** words		
Unit 16 **ou** words		
Unit 17 Commonly misspelt words 1		
Unit 18 Revision		
Unit 19 **th** words		
Unit 20 **sh** words		
Unit 21 **igh** words		
Unit 22 **ch** words		
Unit 23 **le** words		
Unit 24 **oi** words		
Unit 25 Silent letters		
Unit 26 Australian and New Zealand cities		
Unit 27 Revision		
Unit 28 **tch** words		
Unit 29 **soft c** words		
Unit 30 **soft g** words		
Unit 31 **ore** words		
Unit 32 **ie** words		
Unit 33 **er** words		
Unit 34 **tt** words		
Unit 35 Commonly misspelt words 2		
Unit 36 Revision		